D1609786

LATER THAN
WE THOUGHT

'. . . a mean and sordid decade.'

W. H. Auden

A Portrait of The Thirties

LATER THAN WE THOUGHT

René Cutforth

DAVID & CHARLES
Newton Abbot London North Pomfret (VT) Vancouver

ISBN 0 7153 7123 1

Library of Congress Catalog Card Number
76-26733

Set in 11 on 12 point Bembo
and printed in Great Britain
by Alden Press, Oxford
for David & Charles (Publishers) Limited
Brunel House Newton Abbot Devon

Published in the United States of America
by David & Charles Inc
North Pomfret Vermont 05053 USA

Published in Canada
by Douglas David & Charles Limited
1875 Welch Street North Vancouver BC

Contents

1 1930 as a Point in Time *7*

2 Depression *12*

3 The Social Scene *25*

4 Outlook *40*

5 House and Home *51*

6 Politics *59*

7 Marching in Step *66*

8 Entertainment *76*

9 Half-time *94*

10 Royal Occasions *102*

11 The Rehearsal *108*

12 Comings and Goings *114*

13 Waiting for the End, Boys *123*

14 Afterthoughts *131*

100 Thirties People *133*

Events and Entertainments of the Year *141*

Further Reading *153*

Acknowledgements *155*

Index *157*

Groups of unemployed men singing in the gutter, in their proletarian uniform of cloth cap and muffler, had been a feature of the London scene for a long time. Many of them were miners from South Wales. Few passers-by bothered to spare them a glance, let alone a penny. *(Radio Times Hulton Picture Library)*

1 · 1930 as a Point in Time

I was twenty-one in 1930; even before the Wall Street crash of 1929 it had become obvious to me and to friends of mine of my own age that an abrupt change of style was due to arrive with the new decade. I say 'friends of my own age' rather than 'the young' because 'youth', in the contemporary sense of a mass movement in uniform with a mass outlook and a mass sensibility, did not exist between the wars. There never were more than a few hundred of the 'bright young people', and a few thousand of their middle-class imitators in the provinces.

What was true was that the generation which had been born around 1900 was left without any credible landmarks. The gap between them and the rest was suddenly gigantic: it was manifest that their fathers had made a ghastly mess of everything. Civilisation had not perished by an act of God, such as an earthquake or an invasion from Mars. Civilisation had simply failed, and its heirs and assigns, those elder statesmen whose long immersion in the classics and the histories of Rome and Greece had been held to fit them uniquely for the corridors of power, were seen as mere clowns, if not murderers. Wisdom had been their stock-in-trade, and it had not been forthcoming. The confident pronouncements of the Christian clergy were also deeply suspect. It seemed they had been walking, not with God, but with their own conceit and ignorance. And those splendid symbols of the might and majesty of nations, the royal families of old Europe, with their gorgeous uniforms and noble postures, were now revealed in all their nakedness as rather stupid megalomaniacs.

With these three faiths subverted, all values were in the melting-pot. The old social order was a mere shadow of its former self: most of the old landed families had perished in the Flanders mud, or been sold up after the war. Their successors, 'the hard-faced men who looked as if they had done well out of the war', were about as endearing as bloated vultures. So the post-war generation had to rely on its own devices, and these turned out to consist largely of gin and jazz.

I was a member of that rather anxious middle class whose grandparents had been rich, but whose parents (and this was a feature of the time) were doing much less well than they had expected to do, and had no idea how to cope with the new age. I was pretty well placed to give my decade a long appraising look, because the little black coalmining town in the English Midlands where I was born and bred was reduced to desperation by the Depression, and every time I came home from some city where the period's 'glamour' was in evidence, the brutal facts which underlay it were plain to be seen in the lives of people I knew well.

By 1929 the two genuine revolutions of the Twenties, the sex revolution and the filial one, both born of the war, had been very largely successful in the middle class. Young women behaved very much as they liked, to a constant bellowing accompaniment of expostulation and recrimination, and young men no longer expected to hoe that long row of filial obedience and respect which had often carried their fathers well into middle age as dutiful sons.

It seems obvious now that the 'Gay Twenties' were really a shock syndrome, and that much of the shock had been shell-shock. Shell-shock has been defined as 'a condition of alternate moods of high excitement and apathy, with a very quick reaction to sudden emergencies, but no capacity for concentrated thinking'. The condition occurs in nervous sytems saturated with adrenalin due to a long exposure to fear and noise, and – according to Robert Graves, who ought to know – anybody who had endured five months of trench warfare or suffered three rolling artillery barrages was a shell-shock case anyway, though the symptoms might not manifest themselves for a year or two, and it might take five or six more years for the blood to run normal again. So it seems likely that in the Twenties shell-shock was not confined to the few thousand cases noted in the medical records, but ran into many hundreds of thousands at least, and may well have been the prime mover in launching that decade on its long uncaring flight from reality.

Towards its end the blood was clearing up again, and one of the signs of a new hardihood of spirit was a sudden spate of books about the war. All through the Twenties the Great War had been the one impossible subject. Mutual incomprehension between the returning soldiers and the civilians had been absolute: there was no communication and anyway the soldiers preferred to keep quiet. Now suddenly the dumb began to speak and the deaf began to listen. *Goodbye to All That* by Robert Graves, *All Quiet on the Western*

Front by Erich Remarque, *Death of a Hero* by Richard Aldington, and the play *Journey's End* by R. C. Sherriff – all appeared to great acclaim right at the end of the decade. It was a breakthrough for reality: the brilliant, brittle persona which the Twenties had assumed to protect a wounded psyche began to seem redundant – perhaps it was protecting one against life itself. Gin, Jazz and the Jitters had had a long run. As a way of life, had they proved entirely satisfactory? Darling was feeling a tiny bit worn, and now there was a new generation around to emphasise the feeling.

The new generation, mine, the one which was to exhihit the peculiar attitudes and fashions in taste and thought and behaviour which came to be thought of as 'Thirties', was remarkably free of emotional debts. Born around 1910, it carried no burden of nostalgia for the Golden Age before the war, and the war itself had barely touched it. A shadow, not more than that. The song 'There's a long, long trail a-winding' still seems to me to trail an unearthly sadness about it, and I know that that is because I associate it with visits of condolence paid by my mother, very subdued and dressed in black, to weeping ladies in darkened rooms, while I sat in a sailor suit on some stark chair in a corner,

Crowds of desperate investors brought traffic to a halt outside the New York Stock Exchange on the worst day of the Wall Street crash in 1929, which launched the world depression. Police had to be called in to control the situation. *(Associated Press)*

wishing I was anywhere else. Then, at school, there was the odd embarrassing sight of masters in tears on Armistice Day and, even more embarrassing, one of them who dissolved into shaking ruin whenever a car back-fired or the thunder rolled. Their demonic rages at provocations so slight as to be incomprehensible I put down, at the age of thirteen, to the normal human condition, at least in masters, and it was not for another seventeen or eighteen years that I caught up again with men who were 'battle happy' and 'round the bend'.

It left us untouched, but nevertheless it was the war which created the climate of the Thirties. It created the most unbridgeable generation gap of all time. The world in which our parents had disported themselves like fish in water was the world of E. M. Forster and H. G. Wells, and this world had been brutally and suddenly abolished. Fathers and mothers spoke and behaved like people from another world and they were manifestly ill at ease, if not downright incompetent, in this new one. Authority had lost all might, but it never stopped shouting. The Press was feverish in its denunciation of the 'bright young people' and their idiotic goings-on, and every day the bishops, the dons, the headmasters, the politicians, the columnists, the generals, parents and grandparents barked out their demands for a return to Christian worship, decent standards, respectful behaviour, feminine modesty, hard work, sexual repression, more flogging and a sense of duty. Always a 'return' – none of them wanted to go anywhere except backwards. But 1910 had no charms for the young, and particularly not for the young women. They had got out, and they were not going back. The Thirties lot were all about sixteen at the time of the General Strike, and the spectacular meanness and villainy which brought the miners low was not lost on some of them.

Every High Street in the land knew the desolating sound of the cornet as played by small bands of unemployed ex-servicemen shuffling along the kerb. The unemployed, already a national institution, hung about in groups at street corners in the heavy-industry towns and now, at the end of the decade, it was Labour's turn to demonstrate once again that nobody had the faintest idea what to do about unemployment, which had stood at about a million throughout the Twenties. London was still fabulously rich and gay. The youngest women were beginning to wonder whether it was absolutely necessary to look and behave like men in order to be free like men. Organised Labour was still depressed and cowed after its defeat in the Battle of the General Strike, but there were signs that unemployment might be on the decline. The last Diaghilev Ballet season was on at Covent Garden. The 'bright young things' had quite faded away – when on 24 October 1929, like a great clap of thunder in a clear blue sky, the Great American Boom collapsed, and the bottom fell out of the stock market on Wall Street.

All through the Twenties, the American economy had been booming. No such prosperity had ever been thought of: it seemed as if nothing could go wrong. Hundreds of thousands of ordinary American citizens, completely ignorant of finance, took to gambling all their spare cash on stocks and shares, which, in most cases, were rising fabulously. All went merrily for a time, and some of them got rich, and many made money. But the sight of so many innocents at play had been too much for the financiers who now pushed share prices up to the topmost limit – and baled out. In the event, the crash was so spectacular that it pulled the whole house down about their own ears. The Americans who had lost their spare cash dived for the banks to save their capital. The small banks failed and pulled down the big banks, and the USA was on its way to the 'threadbare thirties' as Groucho Marx called them, with sixteen million unemployed. But still the storm held off over Europe. We hoped the Americans would soon recover. It might be bad for trade if they didn't. But 1929 passed into 1930 without undue alarm or despondency, with the barometer somewhere between 'Fair' and 'Unsettled'. It was months before the storm broke.

2 · *Depression*

The depression which followed the Wall Street crash was to extend worldwide, and world trade dropped by nearly a half during the next four years. As industrial production slumped in the sophisticated countries, the demand for its raw materials such as cotton and rubber fell away, so that every kind of national economy was involved.

Unemployment rose sharply in Britain from one million, where it had stayed all through the Twenties, to two million at the end of 1930, and then to very nearly three million in 1932, and it never dropped much below the two million mark until almost the end of the decade. The British got off comparatively lightly – the German figure was six million – but even so for many people, particularly in the old-fashioned heavy industrial towns of the North and Midlands, unemployment became a permanent way of life, sometimes for whole communities.

A Labour Government had succeeded the Conservatives in the 1929 election quite smoothly, as a result of the normal wax and wane of party popularity with the electors. It had been some time since Labour carried the 'Bolshie' tag and Ramsay MacDonald, the new Prime Minister, had introduced the members of his Cabinet as 'chosen for very hard work, and because I believe the nation fully believes they are perfectly competent to perform it'.

In the event, they proved as incompetent as anybody else to stem the tide of unemployment, which only subsided towards the end of the decade in the rearmament programme for the Second World War. J. H. Thomas, the Minister responsible, admitted that he had no clue to the situation, and confessed jokingly that he was breaking all records in unemployment.

At this point, in early 1931, the whole European credit system sustained a near-fatal jolt when the Austrian bank, Kredit Anstalt, failed, and had to be shored up again with, among other splints and bandages, a loan from the Bank of England. There had been a steady drain of gold from the Bank of England ever since the

American loans had ceased to flow into Central Europe, and now the Bank of England asked New York for a loan. It was touch and go. A British Government report had just been published which showed that the Government was overspending by £120 million a year, so the New York bankers refused the loan until Britain had taken steps to balance her budget. Now this was crisis of the ugliest kind because, if the American loan was not forthcoming, the Bank of England might have to default on its obligations and then Britain would have to 'go off the gold standard'. the gold standard was a greatly revered sacred cow in financial circles in those days, and it was believed that to 'go off the gold standard' was automatically to drop the value of your currency almost to zero.

A programme of drastic cuts in Government expenditure was the only answer, and MacDonald and some of his senior colleagues made a plan to reduce the pay of the armed forces, civil servants and school teachers, and to cut unemployment pay by 10 per cent. But now he was in a very tight spot. Although the Opposition said the cuts were too small, half of his own Cabinet refused to accept the cut in unemployment pay. There was much to be said

There were a million substandard houses in Britain, most of them a legacy from the Victorians, built for people who could afford only the minimum of space and had to live within walking distance of the factory. By the Thirties, these houses were thoroughly decrepit and broke the hearts of the women who had to struggle with them. *(Radio Times Hulton Picture Library)*

for their point of view. They were, after all, a Labour government. Unemployment had stood at one million when they took office, and now stood at two and three quarter million: all they had been able to do for the unemployed was to go on paying the 'dole', and the dole was the merest stop-gap between life and death. It would support life only in the sense that it kept people breathing. Throughout the decade one third of the population lived on the poverty line, and one third below it. Even in 1939 it was officially reckoned that a million British houses were substandard. And there remained, a gift from the Victorians, acres and acres of slum terraces – tiny, poky blackened brick boxes for people who could afford to rent only the bare minimum of space and had to live within walking distance of their place of work. No bathroom, of course, and usually no water-closet. Most of these houses shared an earth closet in the yard outside. Quite often not even an interior water tap. To keep clean in such houses the women had to work like navvies with the copper and the copper-stick, the mangle, the range and the great kettles. And the 'children in between': children like the poet George Barker:

> Now I know what was wanting in my youth,
> It was not water or a loving mouth.
> It was what makes the apple-tree grow big,
> The mountain fall, and the minnow die.
> It was hard cash I needed at my root.
> I now know that how I grew was due
> To echoing guts and the empty bag –
> My song was out of tune for a few notes.

So the Labour Cabinet dug in its heels and MacDonald resigned. The cortege which bore the stricken statesman to the Palace to tender his resignation to the King returned in triumph to proclaim (but not until the next day) that MacDonald was still Prime Minister, but now of a 'National Government' composed of Conservatives and Liberals as well as some of his own senior colleagues. In an emergency budget the cuts were duly brought into force by Philip Snowden, the Chancellor, who had followed MacDonald into the new National Government. Sixpence on the income tax, ten per cent on surtax, a penny a pint on beer, teachers' pay reduced by fifteen per cent and Police, Army, Navy and Air Force pay by various drastic cuts. The dole was reduced from seventeen shillings to fifteen and threepence.

That was on 11 September, and on 14 September a naval mutiny

This unemployed man and his family are sitting down to the big meal of the day, boiled fish, dry bread and tea. Many fared worse. At least these children are relatively warmly dressed, and they still have the wireless set. *(Radio Times Hulton Picture Library)*

Ramsay MacDonald leads his colleagues in the 1931 Coalition Cabinet into the back garden of No 10 Downing Street to have their official photograph taken. J. H. Thomas is immediately behind him, and Lord Reading, Stanley Baldwin Philip Snowden follow him down the stairs. *(Radio Times Hulton Picture Library)*

broke out at Invergordon, when the ratings of the warship *Valiant* and two other ships refused to obey the order to put to sea. It was the politest mutiny ever staged and the men refused to acknowledge that it was one: according to them it was a strike. Nobody was hurt or even molested. Respect for officers, except in the matter of obeying their orders, was fully maintained. The few ratings who started to sing 'The Red Flag' were considered to be out of order and in bad taste. The whole enterprise was carried through to the tune of 'The more we are together the merrier we shall be', a popular drinking song, and the ratings themselves instituted a ritual of saluting the White Ensign. Their manifesto, a representation of their case to the Admiralty, read:

> We, the loyal subjects of His Majesty the King, do hereby present to our Lords the Commissioners of the Admiralty our representation and implore them to amend the drastic cuts in pay which have been inflicted on the lowest-paid men of the lower deck. It is evident to all concerned that these cuts are a fore-runner of tragedy, misery and immorality among the families of the lower deck, and unless a guaranteed written agreement is received from the Admiralty, confirmed by Parliament, stating that our pay will be revised, we are still to remain as one unit, refusing to serve under the new rates of pay. The men are quite agreeable to accept a cut which they consider within reason.

As one of the ratings told a reporter: 'We are fighting for our wives and children. The cuts cannot hit us on board ship. We've cut out the luxuries long ago. Our wives, after the rent is paid, have no more than a pound. How can they stand a cut of seven and sixpence?'

The Invergordon mutiny caused no great scandal in Britain, for the simple reason that it was barely mentioned by the British Press, and then only vaguely as some sort of trouble in the Navy. The Admiralty tried to hush up the whole affair, and the result was that only garbled versions and rumours escaped to the foreign press, where they were blown up ten times life size to suggest an ugly and bloody revolutionary rising in the British Navy.

Obviously, if the British Navy was disaffected, Britain was on the road to ruin, and there was another spectacular run on the Bank of England's gold. No doubt it was this consideration which prompted the Government to deal so quickly, sensibly and mildly with the mutiny, reducing the cuts and restoring the status quo almost at once. Twenty-four ratings were dismissed the service, but not until some time later, and that was all – except that the run on the Bank had been so exhausting that the Government which had been formed a few weeks earlier to safeguard the gold standard was now forced to give it up anyway. The pound, instead of crashing to the floor as had been feared, fell to about seventy-five per cent of its former value which, if anything, improved the foreign trade situation.

That was in September, and in October Ramsay MacDonald went to the country, and returned with the biggest parliamentary majority since the passing of the Reform Bill. The National Government was returned with 554 seats, the Labour opposition was reduced to a mere rump of 52 and the Liberals had 16. The country was convinced that the Socialists had brought the pound to the verge of disaster, and it had only been snatched from the very brink by the noble MacDonald, in the role of St George. In the Labour Party, and in Labour circles generally, never has there been such an uproar as broke out at the end of that election, and the wound still rankles just below the surface. No name was too vile for MacDonald and his apostate crew. He was accused of 'betraying his class'. His own party ostracised him, and he never was the friend of the Conservatives who now formed the larger part of his Government. For the rest of his political life he was a tragic, isolated figure, and since he was at heart a warm man who needed sympathy and valued loyalty, this rough handling deeply upset him and was probably responsible for his deterioration as a public figure. MacDonald was a Victorian. His loyalty to 'the Nation' was quite unequivocal. When it was seen by him to conflict with his socialism, it was the socialism that lost out. Though for the rest of his life he was quite sure that he had done his duty by the nation and was unjustly put upon, something in him gave way. He had always aspired to the grand manner in politics, and even then his oratory had always been on the large, vague side; now it grew larger and vaguer with every year in which he visibly aged, until Churchill's brutal remark that his speeches contained 'the smallest amount of thought in the largest number of words' was not an unfair description.

The new Government imposed the means test. Of all the blows

Overleaf

The first act of the new Government was to cut the dole by 10 per cent and to bring in the means test. A protest meeting is developing among the great crowd of disappointed unemployed outside the St Pancras Labour Exchange in London. *(Associated Press)*

PRATTS
NUT BROWN

which fell upon the poor and unfortunate in the Thirties, whether by accident, incompetence or design, this grubby measure was the best calculated to divide the nation and the most bitterly resented. The dole had grown out of the old unemployment insurance benefit when, back in 1921, it had proved inadequate to cope with the new vast scale of unemployment. The unemployment fund had to borrow £30 million from the Treasury, and that became the dole, and a new bureaucracy grew up to administer it. This bureaucracy now enlarged itself to apply the means test. The means test meant that an unemployed man who had come to the end of his insurance stamps was now at the mercy of a Public Assistance Committee, empowered to enquire into every halfpenny that found its way into his house. Officials used to camp out in his front room, poking and prying into all the family's private domestic affairs until there was murder in the air. It was not just a matter of the discovery of concealed or undeclared sources of income, but if one of the children helped with a milk round for a few bob, or ran errands occasionally, or even was spotted wearing a new coat, the dole was adjusted accordingly. Besides the personal indignity, 'the Test', George Orwell said, in *The Road to Wigan Pier*, 'was an encouragement to the tattle-tale and the informer, the writer of anonymous letters and the local blackmailer; to all sorts of unneighbourliness'.

In practice, it raised the status of the clerks and managers who administered the dole from that of suspect and resented bureaucrats to magisterial petty tyrants wielding real power. Too much now depended on their goodwill. Industrial relations probably never recovered from the means test: it was the final snuffer-out of hope in hundreds of thousands of families, many of which were broken up for ever by its impact. I personally knew three families in the little black coal and clay villages of South Derbyshire where, after a year or two of dire poverty with only the mother and the eldest son earning anything at all, Dad was finally told to get out and fend for himself. These had been quite normal, tolerant, decent families: they were done for by the means test.

The chief horror of unemployment lay in the consciousness of an hour by hour expiry of meaningless time. Some gave up early and stayed in bed. In Church Gresley, near my home, the reading room at the public library was always full: all the chairs were occupied a minute after the doors opened, though there was never a queue. Men thought it only decent to lurk round corners or in 'entries' and alleyways until a few seconds after opening time. The brasher spirits, first in, occupied the chairs, and the more hesitant claimed floor space to stand around the high reading stands, where the free newspapers, in the free heating, represented the day's gain. Nobody could afford to smoke – Woodbines were twopence a packet of five – so the 'No Smoking' notices were redundant. The crowd was almost completely silent, and the men all had that slow-wandering eye of those in whom a very low diet had enlarged the faculty of daydreaming. A decade later I was observing the same face, the same slow vagueness, in a prisoner-of-war camp. There was a faint sour smell of unwashed clothes (hot water cost money) and this increased as the day wore on, until by closing time at six o'clock, with the gas hissing as it poured a wash of primrose-coloured light over the dark caps and overcoats and the walls of institution-brown, the fug in the reading room was more than cosy: self-hypnosis, the one true friend of the desperate, had been achieved.

If you had sixpence, you could have a softer seat in the warmer darkness of a cinema and pay Hollywood to do your dreaming for you right up to ten o'clock at night. If you were newly outcast and still vigorous you could go snaring rabbits and hares in the countryside, or join the Communist Party, or even take off on the tramp 'down South', a frighteningly foreign country but relatively free of the great blight.

For there is another aspect of the Thirties which, being undramatic, has no place in song and story: it is that standards of living were actually rising in that black decade. In the Thirties, if you had a job, and particularly if you had it in one of the new light industries, you were not badly off, and your parents' way of life could seem dismally restricted and archaic. It was only the old-fashioned heavy basic industries, the ones which had made Britain's fortune, which were now derelict: in the new industries based on electricity or petrol instead of steam, and consumer goods instead of iron and steel, there was a genuine and rising prosperity. All through the period between the wars the building trade had boomed: indeed, in 1939 one third of all the houses in Britain had been built during the previous twenty years. Plastics appeared in the Thirties, and man-made fabrics, beginning with artificial silk, were going well by the end of the decade. There was a great increase in the employment of women in the new electric and electronic factories, where equally new nimble-fingered techniques proved beyond the scope of the old-fashioned muscular worker, however skilled. Domestic servants, 'the maids', whose reluctance to come forward for employment had provoked so much naive astonishment and indignation in letters to the middle-class Press in the Twenties, were now becoming more and more difficult to get. They now demanded real pay, a day off in the week and tolerable rooms to live in. There was a boom in new 'labour saving' – ie servant eliminating – appliances.

It was in the Thirties that the British middle-class scene turned visibly modern. The huge iron kitchen range had owned a red-faced cook or 'cook-general', often an apt title for a tyrant of the kitchen. When the cook-general failed to appear in her place of duty to be roasted alive at the range until she was properly scarlet, preferring to work in a factory, the range had to go, to be replaced by a gas or electric cooker. This relieved the maids of the desperate weekly chore of black-leading the monster and since, during the decade, hundreds of thousands of people were employed as door-to-door salesmen demonstrating vacuum cleaners, and stainless steel knives came into use, along with electric fires which eliminated most of the coal-heaving, a kitchenfull of girls became more and more of a luxury. Only the copper and the great iron mangle stayed on for years to prolong the penal servitude of the

New, clean, cheerful, well-equipped factories in the clothing and electronics industries attracted women in large numbers. Apart from heavy industry, and despite the pervading depression, the standard of living actually rose during the Thirties. *(Marks & Spencers Ltd)*

past. Americans, it was well known, had washing machines, but only a few of the eccentric and under-bred 'new rich' were hardy enough to transplant them to these sacred shores. For many years after the refrigerator had become standard domestic equipment in the USA, a cold slate slab in the north-east corner of the house where the larder with the gauze window still had its place was the Britons' main line of defence against food poisoning. Every one of those life-lighteners had to be begged, prayed and fought for by women against a strong male rearguard action, which resented each one of them as it arrived as part of a process called 'Americanization', which aimed at destroying good old high-bred British stoicism and the cold bath ethic, and would lead us all into decadence and ruin. It was no accident that one of the earliest pieces of electric equipment to be found around the British home was 'Madam's' hair-dryer.

The new industries which produced these marvels had also produced a new style of worker and greatly augmented the middle class at its lower paid end; it was these people, together with the old middle class of independent shopkeepers, tradesmen and small business men, with the professional upper-middle class, the new financial and managerial upper class and the remnants of the land-owning aristocracy, who could have been expected to vote solidly for the National Government and stability. In the event they were joined by at least half of the old working class who were in such dire straits, and this was a straight vote for tradition: 'in the crisis' it was thought (as it often is in Britain), 'we shall be saved, if at all, by those who are used to ruling and governing according to well-tried formulae which in the past have put us on top'. That was the reason for the huge majority in the House of Commons enjoyed by MacDonald and Baldwin, and by Chamberlain after them.

Everybody in the world except ourselves knows that the British are hypocrites. With the French, who burned Joan of Arc and have ever since accused us of doing it, this is a matter of religious belief, as well it might be, since they pride themselves on their lucidity. British hypocrisy consists of a refusal to formulate in thought or in words an unwelcome proposition, while in the subconscious the mind has already been made up. Put lucidly the proposition before the British nation in the 1930s would run something like this: in the last war nearly a million British men, in the younger half of the population, laid down their lives for King and Country/Civilisation/Freedom. Take your pick. Since we are not at this moment, as we sometimes feared we would be, a bankrupt German province, it can be said that their sacrifice saved us. We are now in the position of having to be saved again. It seems that the sacrifice required this time is that a further one and a half million, the permanently unemployed, lay down their lives, not abruptly and in violence like the soldiers: they will not even have to stop breathing, but 'lives' in the sense in which we want to preserve them in these islands, they cannot have. If this is what has to be, amen.

Put like that, I don't believe the proposition would have won a single vote, but in fact that is the way we voted and that is what happened. To the end of the decade about a million and a half workers were relegated to limbo and their lives laid waste. But not without a struggle.

3 · *The Social Scene*

It is impossible to set the English scene at any period without becoming involved in the subject of class and this is particularly true of the Thirties when, for a variety of reasons, the great English preoccupation was at its most sensitive and complicated. I say 'English' and not 'British' because class in Scotland, Wales and Ireland was and is quite a different thing – in fact, three quite different things.

The strange English mania for subtle social distinctions held onto like grim death is probably derived from the great shock of 1066, which left them a second-class people in their own country. In a sense it might be true to say that the Norman occupation lasted just about nine hundred years, and I fancy I heard its death rattle around the pubs and clubs in London in 1966.

In the beginning it must have been simple enough. The landed aristocracy which had won its land by force of arms at the Battle of Hastings became the top layer under the monarchy, but in England only the eldest male heir inherits the land and the title, so the younger sons were a problem. They could go into the armed services or the Church or, later, into trade, shading off from an upper to an upper-middle class where they met the professions, who shaded off into a middle class, and so on through an infinity of fine gradations. The odd thing is not that this should have happened but that it should have lasted so long and generated so much intensity. Why bother?

The Thirties was an intensely middle-class decade and, for most ordinary people, a reactionary one. When the great economic storms began to blow and the young intellectuals of the upper-class Universities of Oxford and Cambridge – but particularly Oxford – became violently red and revolutionary almost overnight, the middle class rediscovered romantic patriotism. Phrases like 'Our English heritage', 'the Tradition of Empire' and 'the Pageant of History' took a firm place in their hearts. The mass of the people, middle class and working class, who had fought in the war and still hoped against hope for a Merrie England, lined up solidly behind the Pageant of History's living representatives, the Royal family. George V commanded a massive popularity. He was gruff, solid and sensible. He made sensible remarks. Of a member of MacDonald's Government with whom he became friendly, he said 'If I'd had that man's childhood I should feel exactly as he does'. His BBC Christmas broadcasts in which, after a round-up of

The last of the old school of royalty, before the democratic image took over. George V was nevertheless a great rallying point for popular feeling in an age which suddenly rediscovered its 'heritage', and Queen Mary's austere and regal manner was generally acclaimed. *(Paul Popper Ltd)*

voices from all over the Empire, he spoke with great simplicity to his people, made him a father figure. His image was greatly enhanced by the fact that his Hanoverian origins had given him a classless accent.

I don't suppose a million people in England during the Thirties had even heard of the handful of revolutionary poets who are now held to have been the decade's voice. There were other voices far

An elegant woman and a plate of oysters. The West End of London in the Thirties saw itself as the arbiter of a certain well-bred sophistication. It was a great time for the fashionable restaurant. *(Radio Times Hulton Picture Library)*

more characteristic of the time, at the time, and one of them belonged to Richard Tauber. There can scarcely have been a single hour of any day during the Thirties when the voice of Richard Tauber was not to be heard somewhere in England, singing 'You are my heart's delight'. That voice, sentimental, Teutonic, full-bloodedly romantic, lands you right in the middle of the Thirties, into a world of small-town snobberies and careful class discriminations, of golfing tweeds worn mainly by people who never played golf. Plus-fours, a sort of very full pair of knickerbockers worn over woollen stockings in diamond patterns, with tufted woollen garters, grew with the decade into enormous deformities, like Dutchmen's folk breeches. In the end the golfers for whom plus-fours were designed gave them up, when they became the hallmark of a certain kind of beefy young man leaping from a beetle-sized open sports car into the saloon bar of the new Tudor pub in the suburbs, or even one of the drinking and dancing palaces on the new by-pass roads, which were called roadhouses. There was a very famous one on the Kingston by-pass called the Ace of Spades where the Prince of Wales could sometimes be seen, to the grave disapproval of the middle-aged and the rapture of the new middle-class young, who felt he had gone out of his way to identify himself with them.

It was the slicker breed of sports car which drove up to the roadhouse – a three-litre Bentley, perhaps, in the dark green of England's racing team, with a strap round the bonnet. There was more champagne than bitter drunk at the Ace of Spades but, all the same, it was considerably unbuttoned for that period: almost anybody could get in there so long as he had his hair appropriately slicked back with Brylcreem – or the even better-known Anzora Viola, a highly scented product – with perhaps a little Ronald Colman moustache, a single-breasted flannel jacket, a pair of not too outrageous plus-fours. If you were a 'lounge lizard', in which type the cult of the smooth and languid was brought to its pitch of perfection, you sported a little pair of sideburns, not woolly but clipped and smooth like dabs of tar; and all young men, not only lounge lizards, set great store by a whole armoury of personal paraphernalia, cufflinks, cigarette holders, cigarette cases, studs and tie pins. They all meant much more than they have done since and most of these gadgets were counters in the class game.

Cloth caps were the correct thing to wear with plus-fours, but a good deal of care went into the shaping of these to lift them very noticeably above the level of the proletarian cloth cap which was almost universal among the workers, young and old – even some of the women: in the North and Midlands, stout middle-aged women trudged to and fro with jugs of beer, their cloth caps skewered on with a foot of savage hatpin.

By 1934 the social scene varied extremely in different parts of the country. The West End of London was obviously rich and prosperous, a glitter of plate-glass windows with all that was best in the world's loot on elegant display behind them. Fashionable clothes were still formal in the Thirties: top hats, striped trousers and morning coats were still worn by those who took their appearance seriously as a matter of social duty. Rolls-Royces glided about among restaurants which paid £20,000 every three years for a complete face-lift by whoever was in the ascendant in the world of interior decoration, a very fashionable occupation. At the entrances to the great hotels, and a good many more which mushroomed into fashion and then died, a special race of highly sophisticated hall-porters in fancy liveries could distinguish at a glance those who had always taken their privileges for granted from those who were newly rich and those temporarily in the money, and vary their manner accordingly.

All this movement towards bourgeois relaxation was in high contrast with the political developments among the intellectuals. As they grew daily more violently red and austere, the mainstream culture relapsed cosily into warm sentimentality, traditional loyalties and nostalgia.

In the North, the black industrial towns were now little better than grim prisons, where whole populations served their time without even the alleviation of knowing how long their sentence was to last. Faith had gone long since, but hope never quite expired.

It was in the High Streets of small towns, mostly in the southern half of England, that the normal life of the country pursued its unexciting and snobbish course. It was not a bad life, an improvement on that of the previous decade, because mass-production had by now achieved some of its miracles. Prices were very low in Britain. In the High Street, the office worker could have a three-course lunch for one shilling (5p), and if he liked to spend one shilling and threepence, one of the courses could be steak and onions with chips. There was a Woolworths in almost every High Street, where everything cost sixpence or less. This phrase needs a little interpretation. A kettle, for instance, cost sixpence, and its lid cost sixpence; you could buy a pair of spectacles: the frame cost sixpence, and each lens cost sixpence and you tested your own eyes with a card on the counter. Woolworths was exciting, like a treasure chest. You could set up housekeeping from Woolworths; and with cups and saucers at twopence apiece you catch a ghastly glimpse of the life-style of the unemployed, who spent so much of their time making cups from condensed milk tins, and patching up the kettle with the same material.

Montague Burton, the Tailor of Taste, lived in the High Street, too. He could fit you out with a good suit for fifty shillings. It would invariably have a waistcoat for the interesting reason that trousers had not then achieved that snug-to-the-waist cut which keeps them up nowadays, so they were kept up by a pair of braces – suspenders, in the United States. But braces were 'low' and 'common': you could not be seen in braces. Hence the waistcoat, though more often than not, if the occasion warranted the smallest degree of informality and you were under fifty, you opted for a Fair Isle pullover. These had originated on a Scottish island as a folk fashion in knitting, and carried gay patterns in bright reds,

On certain fixed days during the London Season you could be sure of seeing the upper class in full fig. This is the Eton and Harrow match at Lord's Cricket Ground in 1933. Parents – and sisters particularly – were expected to cut a dash. *(Radio Times Hulton Picture Library)*

blues and yellows, usually on a fawn ground. They had long since been mass-produced: it was a notable stroke of the universal one-upmanship to own a genuine Fair Isle sweater.

Shirts were white in the Thirties and usually had soft collars with long points, which were joined together under the knot of the tie by a thin gold tiepin. It was a social error if this tiepin had a twisted bar or a round bar or a silver bar: it must be flat and gold. Most of the male population still wore the old clinging 'long John's' under their trousers, though short pants and sports shirts in the new cellular materials like the famous 'Aertex' were rapidly coming into fashion, for – as the Thirties progressed – they developed a fanatical regard for the romantic and therapeutic values of fresh air.

Working men wore boots, and on Sundays these were brown and went with a blue serge suit. Otherwise, except among the over fifties, shoes were the rule. Ties were subdued except when they

West End night clubs, though then considered the acme of sophistication, would today seem very sleazy joints indeed. The chief thrill was cocking a snook at the restrictions on the sale of drink after certain hours, enforced, ever since the war, by the Defence of the Realm Act. *(Radio Times Hulton Picture Library)*

The plus-four suit in hairy tweed, worn with cloth cap, brown shoes and thick woollen stockings, was the fashion which replaced the would-be decadent, Noel-Coward-in-a-dressing-gown, image of the late Twenties. Originally designed for golf, it became the uniform of the hearty and athletic young. *(The Mansell Collection)*

The industrial towns of the North which had made Britain's fortune during the nineteenth century were by now, in the slump, little better than grim prisons where unemployment had become a way of life, and living conditions remained starkly Victorian. *(Radio Times Hulton Picture Library)*

referred to something special such as your old school, your old regiment or your cricket club, in which case they came in diagonal stripes in furious colours. There had been something ladylike about the young men of the Twenties, with their snakelike silhouettes and swirling 'Oxford bags'. The new young men, with their hair plastered down and militarily 'short back and sides', seemed to wish to display assurance, possibly because their circumstances contained so little of it.

One of the things that strikes me most about the Thirties scene when I think about it now is the trilby hat, the universal headgear of the middle class. The trilby was named after the girl in George Du Maurier's novel of the same name, and her hat must have been one of the broad-brimmed, high-crowned artists' hats of the Quartier Latin in Paris. So, sometime early in the century, it must have been a wild gesture of freedom and informality among all those stiff and proper toppers and bowlers. Originally it had been a hat which didn't give a damn. By the Thirties it had certainly become degenerate. It was still broader in the brim than hats are now but not very much and, perhaps symbolically, the crown had been lowered to a dwarfish level. It was a hat which had lost all aspiration: it had become a mingy hat and there was a mingy expression to match it. I thought at first, as I watched on old film those faces underneath those thousands of nearly identical trilby hats, that it was the mean outline of the hat itself which lent the faces the curiously self-contained and calculating look. In the end, I was quite sure that there was a Thirties face, a Thirties expression. It had something to do with the military phrase 'all present and correct' and it went with an assessing, a sitting-in-judgement eye. Nowadays, except for ideologists, we live in an off-stage period like actors having a drink between the acts, but in the Thirties you were on stage the whole time and tense with the effort of playing the part of a thoroughly relaxed and secure individual.

The universal game was class assessment and judgement, as it had been in England for a very long time. You presented your 'all present and correct' act for inspection, and duly inspected the inspector. I think it's true to say, though it makes me sad to think of it, that for millions of people in England in the Thirties, to score well at this game was the chief reason for existence. Probably the reason for the intensity of the feeling for gentility at that time was that the old order of society was seriously crippled. The First World War had slaughtered the upper class in droves and been the financial ruin of most of those who survived. During the Twenties

The High Street vision of the correct. Note the trilby hat, the spats, the cane, the gloves and, above all, the price. The door is mock baronial-gothic, the tie is mock Public School, the moustache is mock military. Cut-price snobbishness is the informing spirit. *(Burton Menswear)*

The pavements of Portsmouth in 1939. There was always a crowd round the doorways of Woolworths. The invasion of the provincial High Street was a Thirties development and, to most people, a welcome one. The clothes of working class children are still noticeably shapeless. *(Radio Times Hulton Picture Library)*

Listening to the band in the Park on a summer's day. Uniformed children's nurses were a feature of the London scene. The man nearest the camera is wearing the boater hat he wore as a youth. By the Thirties boaters were no longer commonly worn, though there were more of them about than there are today. *(Barnabys Picture Library)*

they managed to keep up a much-diminished round of coming-out balls for debutantes and great receptions and dinner parties, reported respectfully in the press, while the fatuous goings-on of their younger generation, the 'bright young things', were the staple diet of the columns in the popular newspapers. They had become a raree-show, and by the Thirties were well on their way to their final destination as an easy-mannered set of horse-copers.

With the upper class more or less relegated, like Red Indians, to reservations (mostly in Scotland), the middle classes took over the administration of English example and precept. In their hands, gentility became a furious competition. Any one of a million tiny indications could exclude you permanently from the sacred enclosure. Things to do with voice and accent, of course, ever since Arnold of Rugby; strange arbitrary rules about clothes: parti-coloured shoes excluded you at once until the Prince of Wales began to wear them; certain colours in clothes – brown suits, for instance – were anathema; and what you did with your cigar-bands was a serious social matter. In the higher echelons of social feeling it mattered greatly, in pouring a cup of tea, whether the milk or the tea went in first. The rules about the wearing of ties were as intricate as English common law and, like it, largely a matter of precedent. What made the game more complicated was that different middle-class sections played it by different rules. In the matter of what was done and what was not done, every white-collared Englishman daily walked a tightrope over a deadly chasm. And you can see this on old newsfilm, as they strut smartly about under their trilby hats.

Women played this game too but, unless they were upper class, not with the zest and vigour which men brought to it. Women's judgements on human beings had more of a biological than a social bias, and besides they had recently staged one of their grand transformation scenes. The old Twenties air of raffish individuality allied with a cool, if gin-soaked, alienation was on the way out, along with the slate-pencil silhouette, the cloche hat, the cropped hair and the long cigarette holder. Breasts, hips and bottoms made a sudden and welcome comeback to the rapturous applause of their old fans, and this coincided with the introduction of the permanent wave. Overnight, it seemed, there was scarcely a straight-haired woman with any pretensions to fashion to be seen throughout the length and breadth of the kingdom: dresses became longer as curves came in again and clothes were suddenly very soft and pretty, even fussy, and crepe de chine was the fashionable material.

These were middle-class fashions. The upper class bought its clothes in Paris or Savile Row. The working class had not enough money to affect fashion at all. It was this middle class at its upper end, narrow, insular, patriotic and responsible, which ran the Empire – and whose public showman throughout the decade was Noel Coward. This was an odd platform for Coward to find himself on. All through the Twenties he had been building up that decade's image as one of alienated unshockability and elegant wickedness – 'what else could you expect, poor things?' But now those clipped accents, that dark-brown, semi-strangulated voice, indicative of reality forcing its way through heavy tides of emotion, was to be at the service of middle-class patriotism and nostalgia. *Cavalcade* was staged in 1931, and followed the fortunes of an upper-middle-class family in England since before the War. In the end, the old couple rose to drink a toast to their King and Country and to patriotic nostalgia in general. This piece was rapturously received and became a sort of testament to the new middle-class feeling. It is believed in theatrical circles, or at any rate it is said, that Coward set out to write *Cavalcade* in a spirit of mockery: it was meant to take the mickey out of the whole middle-class concept of patriotism, the sacrifice of war, the pageant of history, the Royal Family and all the loyalties which bound them to the concept of 'England'. Halfway through, it is alleged, like St Paul he saw a great light, and decided with tears to play it straight. However it came about, from that time on he was the Establishment's adored PRO and his Empire ballad 'Mad dogs and Englishmen go out in the midday sun' was as revered an anthem to the upper-middle class of the period as 'The Red Flag' is to the Labour Party.

With hindsight, anyone can see from here that the Empire had already begun to totter on its foundations but it didn't look like that at the time; though the great days of total assurance with Kipling as High Priest were long over, when the cold winds of economic disaster began to blow in the Thirties the Empire was one of the symbols of their identity which the British clung to with particular affection. About three-quarters of a population in which three million families were on the hunger-line lined up solidly behind the Royal Family, the Empire and the whole archaic patchwork quilt of what was called 'our heritage'. It was a remarkable feat, presided over by Mr Baldwin who seemed to do absolutely nothing sometimes for years on end and then, just at the moment when it seemed that the whole thing must go down the drain, he would rise from his slumbers and give out a kind of pastoral symphony about Old England and the novels of Mary Webb, and the storm would subside at once.

There was, all the same, an autumn air about the Thirties. We were certainly not going forward, and we had not yet begun to retreat. It seems to me, now, as if the British people were driven to stage a kind of recapitulation of their history in romantic terms while these still seemed relevant. There is no doubt that Englishmen of that period felt extremely English, and they liked the feeling. Abroad, except in the Empire, they felt utterly disorientated. To Americans the sacred class assessment and judgement game was a joke which could keep them in stitches all night or, a bit further out from New York, a shameful and wicked state of mind which their Revolution had pronounced anathema.

On the Continent, nobody had the remotest idea what it was all about, and consequently their cultures could not be taken seriously. Continental life, instead of being based on sound rules – such as whether a man was a cad or not, and why – seemed to revolve largely round sex, by which they did not mean Richard Tauber and 'You are my heart's delight' but something quite different which you would have thought their nannies would have told them to beware of. Eating and drinking took far too much of their attention from serious matters, and quite ordinary people were apt to rave on about Art.

It was a naive, innocent, stuffy age and suffered from megalomania. All through the decade, the power of British influence in the world was greatly over-estimated in the British Isles. The Government was always being called upon to stop something over which it had not the remotest control. Even when Oxford undergraduates voted that in no circumstances would they fight for King and Country, they took it for granted that the world would tremble. The country was full of lunatics collecting signatures for one cause or another. If there were enough British signatures against the Big, Bad Wolf it would simply go away.

But what I remember best about the England of the Thirties was the face of the countryside. Most country people lived almost exactly as they had done in 1880. England, most of England, looked much as it had looked in the eighteenth century, and it was very beautiful. The face of England turned out to be the most persuasive poet of them all. It was the author of all that romantic oratory about the Pageant of History, the Common Heritage and the English Tradition which uplifted the people and persuaded them all to ignore the facts of life and to vote the wrong way all through the decade.

4 · Outlook

'Lives there a man with soul so dead
He was not, in the Thirties, Red?'

Perhaps the chief difference of outlook between one period of historic time and another lies in its anxieties and though, in the Thirties, the future often looked black enough, its shadows did not include the atomic bomb and the prospect of instant annihilation, nor the poisoning of the planet by chemical pollution, or the prospect of standing-room only threatened by the population explosion. We were much more parochial than anybody can be in the television age, but also much more metropolitan. It was assumed that the planet could look after itself and the most foreign to the Thirties mind of all subsequent concepts would have been that of the 'global village'. In the Thirties new concepts and ideas did not spread outwards from local prophetic oracles but downwards from the old universities, Oxford and Cambridge; the front line of consciousness, where the present pushed against the frontiers of the future, was in London: it might also be in Paris, New York, Rome or Berlin, but anyway it was metropolitan. In Britain, if you wanted to be where the ideas of the future were being hammered out, London was the place. London was where you met the intellectuals or 'avant garde' or, as the Left preferred to call it, the 'intelligentsia': they had re-located every organ in the body politic and redefined it with a new, antiseptic name.

It was a strange and disorderly mob, the 'intelligentsia', made up of intellectuals and artists and their disciples, sympathisers and hangers-on, and it included a fair number of the rich and fashionable and *their* hangers-on, who found the company less boring than the Establishment. It was, in fact, smart, and also highly alcoholic and paranoid: a sense of persecution was not the main message, yet, but merely a spin-off from other activities. In the Thirties this layer of the population went violently Red almost overnight.

The new mood was born at Oxford University and led by its young poets, Wyston Auden, Stephen Spender, Cecil Day Lewis and, a little later, Louis MacNeice. They were called the 'Auden

Group' but all they had in common was a frame of mind – outrage at the plight of the poor and the smugness of the rest. They launched the revolutionary movement which was to create the most characteristic intellectual climate of the time, and from the start Auden's was the voice of the decade. What they were after was old-fashioned Soviet-type Red revolution. It was to arrive with 'the death of the Old Gang, the death of us'. Auden always sounded as if ten thousand revolutionaries were fighting to snatch his words from the press as they appeared. In fact the audience was so small that it often seemed that these young men were writing their poems to each other. It was just possible in the early Thirties to believe that social justice was flowering in the Soviet Union and that Man was on his way to the millennium by way of Moscow, but only to addicts of belief and these were the Thirties' most

W. H. Auden (right) and Christopher Isherwood, just before they left for China in 1938. Auden was the leader of the group of young Marxist poets who are now held to have been the new voice of the period. *(Radio Times Hulton Picture Library)*

PRICE 3d. No. 35 MAR. 1939

THE LEFT NEWS

EDITED BY VICTOR GOLLANCZ

THE THIRD GREAT ANNUAL RALLY

ACLAND
ANGELL
CRIPPS
THE DEAN
GOLLANCZ
LLOYD GEORGE
POLLITT
ROBERTS
ROBESON
STRACHEY

See page 1189

Victor Gollancz was the indefatigable prophet and publicist of the Left throughout the Thirties. On the cover of this influential periodical, among a covey of politicians, Gollancz represents letters, the Dean (Dean Hewlett Johnson, Dean of St Paul's) religion, and Paul Robeson the theatre.

characteristic product. At all events, the Soviet Union was the sacred cow during the whole decade, and any word of criticism of it was no mere disagreement or even heresy, but rank blasphemy. Most of the intellectuals of the Left were far too 'committed' to bother to get the facts right, and later plenty of them dismissed the Stalin terror brightly as 'necessary for the creation of the new order'. The Thirties was the great age of illusion. In the Thirties they could believe anything.

The Marxists expected the Revolution any week now. Capitalism was supposed to be on its last legs, to have at most a few tottering years to run. One good push would topple it over, and then 'Forward through chaos and catastrophe':

> Drug nor isolation will cure this cancer.
> It is now or never the hour of the knife,
> The break with the past, the major operation.

wrote Day Lewis, and he was speaking for his time. The idea of the 'necessary chaos' was the notion underlying all the art of the Thirties. The revolution was seen by Auden in the coolest terms. The artist's private sensibility, according to him, was no longer relevant: a poet should be 'absolutely detached, like a surgeon or a scientist'. Poetry was to be classical and austere:

> Financier, leaving your little room
> Where the money is made but not spent,
> You'll need your typist and your boy no more;
> The game is up for you and for the others,
> Who, thinking, pace in slippers on the lawns
> Of College Quad or Cathedral Close,
> Who are born nurses, who live in shorts,
> Sleeping with people and playing fives.
> Seekers after happiness, all who follow
> The convolutions of your simple wish,
> It is later than you think.

'It is later than you think' might have been the motto of the whole group.

Throughout the decade George Orwell, whose masterpieces were still to come, made ugly faces at the orthodox Soviet-worshippers and particularly at the Auden Group whom he regarded as divorced from humanity: they had never met anybody not in their own social class, he said, and this annoyed them greatly because he was right.

Picasso's 'Guernica', the most famous painting of the age. The Spanish Civil War aroused violent feelings among artists and intellectuals, and this picture went on tour to gain support for the forces of the Left. *(Museum of Modern Art, New York)*

The political achievements of these poets were very limited. They were exciting at the time: they wrote well: they were genuine poets, but most genuine when least political. They brought some water into the desert of national complacency but not enough to make it flower. They did an admirable and edifying hatchet job on middle-class cant and cowardice, but the comment of another Thirties writer makes a valid point: Peter Quennell wrote: 'The artist who aspires to be a political force seems to completely misunderstand the nature of the art he practises . . . Between writers who have helped to change the world and writers who have set out to change it, there exists a very sharp distinction.'

Far more effective politically was Victor Gollancz's Left Book Club whose sixty thousand readers each received a book a month, chosen by Gollancz and two Marxist intellectuals. It was not necessary to be a Communist or even a Socialist to be on 'the Left' in the Thirties. There was a large, vague area of opinion which called itself 'anti-fascist', a title which included almost everybody who was excited by ideas at all – not very many in Britain at any time – and it was to these 'anti-fascists' that the Left Book Club addressed itself. The books used to arrive sometimes with excited messages attached – 'Terribly urgent!' They held meetings at the Albert Hall to support the Spanish Republicans, urge a popular front, protest against the Japanese invasion of China, which no-one could do anything about. It was an effective propaganda machine and the Communists were its eager beneficiaries.

The ideas propagated by Auden & Co and the Left Book Club

filtering down through the little magazines on railway bookstalls and the lectures of Army Education Corps instructors during the war could probably claim a share in one political victory – the defeat of Churchill in 1945. Their chief influence on their own decade was to ensure that it was against a strong background of the theories of Karl Marx that the other major influences in the

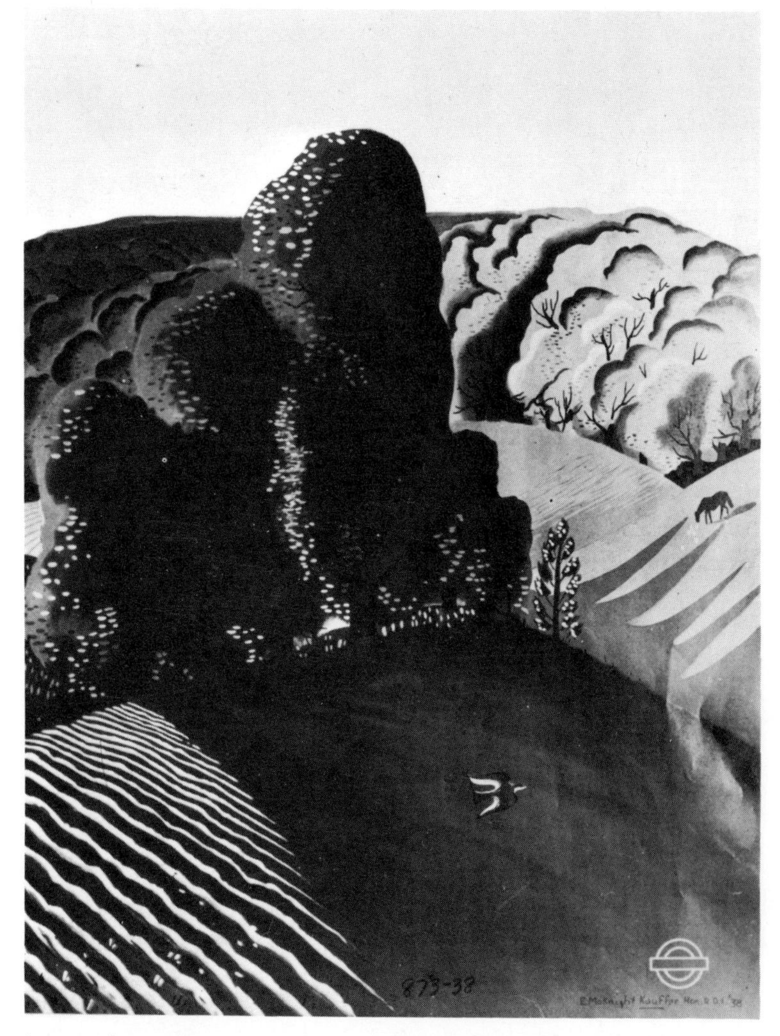

A poster for London Transport by McKnight Kauffer (1938). Posters of this type familiarised the general public with some of the new styles in painting and design and became enormously popular. London Transport was noteworthy for its enlightened policy in all design matters. *(London Passenger Transport Board)*

Thirties had to make themselves felt.

Next to Marx, the chief prophet of the age was Sigmund Freud. The truly orthodox Marxists laid down the law that you couldn't be a Marxist and a Freudian. The governing forces of life had either to be collective and economic or individual and libidinous, not both. And this was typical of the warring ideological sects of the period: there must be no watering down of the sacred word – choose your saviour, Marx or Freud. It was not an ecumenical age. Nevertheless, the two managed a wary cat-and-dog co-existence in many minds of the period. Freud's theory that neurosis was born of the repression of instincts was a godsend to the avant garde. It was freely translated to mean that if your slightest sexual itch was not immediately gratified, your health would suffer and you would probably end in a loony bin. Sex on doctor's orders was the new idea and it did much to reinforce the message of the various brands of sexual missionaries dedicated to freeing the British from their inhibitions. Sex was the cure for everything. There isn't any doubt in my mind that the British of the time were more inhibited sexually than most other Europeans, but the ministrations of these enthusiasts in stripping sex of its romantic trappings – and indeed of any feeling at all except physical excitement – produced about as many casualties as cures. Later in the decade women's fashions produced a round hat in black felt of exactly the cut and shape of a parish priest's. This was the 'Puritan' hat, and originally indicated that its wearer was a bigoted fanatic dedicated to sex in its purest and most clinical form, unadulterated by any other kind of feeling whatever, a high priestess of the erotic.

That prophet Jung, the inventor of 'extroverts' and 'introverts', and the theory of the 'collective unconscious', also established a large influence on the more intellectual writers and readers, but his rather bloodless ideas could not compete with Freud's sexual obsessions in the new popular enthusiasm for psychology.

There was one other prophet of weight in the Thirties and genuinely in revolt against everything they stood for; D. H. Lawrence had died in 1930 but his influence grew throughout the decade. The sexual missionaries claimed him as an ally, but he detested and disowned them. He was on the side of intuition against intellect, of feelings against concepts, of the sense of touch against the kingdom of the eye. Instinct, in his view, had been humbled and bossed about by the mind for far too long: it was time it staged a comeback. Everybody, he said, was dying of over-consciousness; half of their identity – and the most valuable half – and been elbowed off the board of directors and disaster was going to be the consequence. Certainly it was time that somebody pointed out that the detached head had been given altogether too long a run for its money and had reached a stage where it simply didn't notice what it could not be articulate about, but enough's enough and, in my view, the 'dark instincts', together with the sociologists, have more than redressed the balance since then.

But in his own time and immediately after, Lawrence's was a minority voice. It was, in general, typical of the Thirties to feel that the search for reality was a stripping process, simply a matter of getting rid of what was irrelevant. Ever since the beginning of the century, when the artists discovered that underneath the surface of the visible world were forms and patterns of a simpler and more significant nature – more significant, that is to say, to painters and sculptors – art had progressively relinquished the natural object in favour of ideas suggested by the natural object. During the Twenties when Clive Bell was the accepted art pundit in England, some distorted ghost of the original model still usually glimmered faintly in the picture, but by the Thirties as interpreted

The back streets of Bolton in 1938 provide William Coldstream with a subject which makes a social comment as well as a painterly point. Under the influence of Auden he had abandoned abstract painting for a less introverted realism. *(National Gallery of Canada, Ottawa; gift of the Massey Foundation 1946)*

by the new pundit, Herbert Read, the object had disappeared altogether and forms were created which were self-sufficient and existed without reference to any particular object in Nature's world, as concepts, not percepts. The Marxists used to get very excited about this tendency, which they said was a flight from reality and an indication that no artist of sensibility and integrity could relate himself to the capitalist world.

While the poets were busy disclaiming their private sensibilities, the visual arts seemed to take a dive in the opposite direction, into the artist's interior. While for most people Art meant Augustus John and the Royal Academy, or perhaps Stanley Spencer whose picture of the dead rising from their tombs in a country churchyard on Doomsday was a great popular hit, young painters were experimenting with every kind of Continental art movement of the last twenty years. The chief influences were, as always, French. Cubism, invented twenty years before by Picasso and Braque, was concerned with the underlying geometric structure of forms. This was a main pre-occupation of Ben Nicholson, the leader of avant-garde painting in England. He was the most fertile and the most restless of the painters and seems, in retrospect, to have done more for painting than any other native. The British avant-garde was always ten years behind the French, and the British public ten years behind them. But this situation was improving as far as the public were concerned because fashion sketches and advertisements were catching on to new ideas, and McKnight Kauffer's great series of posters in the Underground familiarised the public with the styles of Impressionism and Post-Impressionism, at least, and made them acceptable. Ben Nicholson seemed to want to do the same service for the avant-garde. He would form a group and, the moment it seemed set in its ways, he would leave it with its more active minority and form another. Most of his work was abstract and much of it very exciting. Wyndham Lewis, who had the Italian futurists as models for his Vorticism earlier in the century, was now painting angular up-to-date portraits of his angular up-to-date friends. Wyndham Lewis, who was a writer as well as a painter, and satirised the 'trendies' of his time, was usually referred to by the Left as a Fascist, not that he was one. Early Surrealists like Chirico had conveyed a sense of impending doom which was very fetching in the Thirties and his paintings, or their reproductions, were more likely to be found actually on the walls of advanced young people than later works. Paul Nash created his own, very English, haunted atmosphere of anxiety. Thoroughly English, too, were Graham Sutherland's studies of limestone quarries, though they may have owed something to German Expressionism which was just beginning to bite in England. The new young sculptors, Henry Moore and Barbara Hepworth, halfway between the surrealist and the abstract, though strange were comprehensible.

In Russia, Soviet Realism was the only fashion, and the whole place was plastered with posters of intensely solid workers hammering among cog-wheels with expressions of Napoleonic will-power on their muscular faces. Towards the end of the decade in Britain there was a selfconscious return to realism in the arts. There had always been realist painters about but now, with William Coldstream and the so-called Euston Road School, Realism was suddenly seen as the main line of development, in tune with the social ferment outside. Auden had persuaded Coldstream that abstract painting was a silly game in view of the imminent establishment of the People's Soviet Republic of Britain, but he didn't need much persuading. He had worked along with other painters, poets and composers in the new documentary film movement and had been directly influenced by it.

But the Marxist-Realists were only one small facet of the art scene. The brilliant 'isms' proliferated in the visual arts, while the poets and writers had had about as much as they could take of personal analysis and were disappearing into the Communist Party or the Catholic Church or any solid organisation which seemed to promise a synthesis. In a poem called 'Eclogue for Christmas' Louis MacNeice gives voice to this spiritual fatigue of the Thirties, and ties it in with the never-ceasing jazz accompaniment of the age; an urban character is speaking:

> Jazz-weary of years of drums and Hawaiian guitar,
> Pivoting on the parquet I seem to have moved far
> From bombs and mud and gas, have stuttered on my feet
> Clinched to the streamlined and butter-smooth trulls of the
>   elite,
> The lights irritating and gyrating and rotating in gauze –
> Pomade-dazzle, a slick beauty of gewgaws –
> I who was Harlequin in the childhood of the century,
> Posed by Picasso beside an endless opaque sea,
> Have seen myself sifted and splintered in broken facets,
> Tentative pencillings, endless liabilities, no assets,
> Abstractions scalpelled with a palette-knife
> Without reference to this particular life,
> And so it has gone on; I have not been allowed to be

Myself in flesh or face, but abstracting and dissecting me
They have made of me pure form, a symbol or a pastiche,
Stylised profile, anything but soul and flesh:
And that is why I turn this jaded music on
To forswear thought and become an automaton.

The public reaction of doubt and dismay on first encountering Epstein's work is writ large on these faces. These old ladies are meeting his 'Adam' for the first time. *(Radio Times Hulton Picture Library)*

5 · *House and Home*

In the pop scene – though it had no such name then, but all those jazz-based tunes from America amounted to a genuine pop culture – everybody hummed and whistled those tunes; in that world nobody had the slightest objection to forswearing thought and somewhat debased versions of all those 'isms' presided over the interior decoration of the period. The stepped pyramid, or Ziggurat, was a favourite form. It appeared endlessly in the wide friezes above the pale distempered walls which had superseded flowered wallpaper in middle-class houses. Everything which could look Cubist did, and the Vorticists had contributed those jagged shapes like conventional lightning flashes, usually made of glass, of which most contemporary lampshades were composed. But anything went, from the Art Nouveau which had flourished at the beginning of the century, through the whole range of irritable 'isms' which had been reducing life to its components ever since then. It was all supposed to register vitality, but the effect was often more galvanic than vital. Orange was the decorator's colour of the period: usually orange and black together, but almost any colour with black would do. Zebra skins came in at one time, but the hair falls out of zebra skins, they go bald, and they went out again.

The Regency period supplied the inspiration for the most opulent style of the time. It had itself been based on ancient Greek and Egyptian models, and the Thirties versions were quite often a genuinely successful imitation of the lightness and elegance of the best of the originals. But Regency was very expensive and, like everything else in the Thirties, it was tied in with an ideology. Some of the rich displayed their Regency decor in the spirit of

Overleaf
Any of these objects, nearly all incompatible in style, could have been found together in any smart middle-class home of the Thirties, exercising their primary function of making the owner feel up to date. Some of the forms claim to be austere, but the general effect is both cluttered and cosy. *(Heal & Son)*

'après moi le deluge', a last gesture of a defiant aristocracy before it was overrun by the people, and these sometimes scored a greater success with the Nazi Ambassador Ribbentrop than with the natives of these islands.

But among ordinary people plastics had begun their career in the home in the form of Bakelite, which in the early days was remarkably ugly, cast either in that chocolate brown which rendered schools, prisons and other institutions so depressing at the time, or mottled like the cover of a penny notebook. Light fittings, switches and wireless sets were mostly in Bakelite – and of course the wireless set was the centrepiece in most homes, with its great red-hot valves like an electric fire. By the Thirties the horn-shaped loudspeakers had gone and the whole apparatus was housed in one box, often with a romantic picture in fretwork to form the front and cover the loudspeaker, and in the better-off middle-class homes the wireless and the gramophone were combined in one cabinet to form a contemporary piece of furniture called a radiogram.

Thirties furniture, angular and ugly, was meant to have a 'structural look'. The guru con-man of the period was not the sociologist as at present, but the psychiatrist; everything was not only itself but symbolic of something else – even the ordinary colours and materials. The bright bluish metal chromium began its fashionable run in the Twenties, but it was still going strong in the Thirties. Chromium, arty girls implored you to agree, was 'hard and clean', and a magic charm against the silver teapot culture of the upper class, and the middle-class cosiness of copper. Everything from teapots to cigarette cases was cubical if possible and, if not, angular. This symbolised the discarding of sentiment and other inessentials. We had to get down to the bony structure. Among intellectuals and particularly writers, the colour red was deeply suspect: it represented passion, the reactions of the gut – you were expected to be above and in charge of the reactions of your guts. The sense of touch was out, too. Sight was the superior sense, the eye was the aristocrat of the sense organs. Green was the preferred colour, the colour of the intellect. White was the dreaded badge of innocence, unguardedness, simplicity and the blind.

The towns of Britain greatly changed their appearance between the wars: in the twenty years between 1919 and 1939 four million houses were built and the towns spread outwards in all directions. Most of it was private enterprise building and the outer suburbs today are still quite largely a legacy of the Thirties.

The old Victorian and Edwardian terrace house was a dreary

home, long and narrow and dark, with a tiny front garden in which nothing would grow after the hedge had been planted, and a very narrow strip at the back giving a view of countless others of the same sort. But, quite apart from being cramped and dark and inconvenient, it had the intolerable disadvantage that coal had to be delivered through the house, and if you owned a motor bike that had to go through the door and down the passage and out at the

This bedroom has it all. On the upholstery the influence of McKnight Kauffer is plain to be seen, and the dressing table is functional, labour-saving and sparely designed. The lamp was one of the good Thirties innovations, but the cigarette box and toilet articles come straight from Hollywood. *(Heal & Son)*

back. So the new semi-detached house was very popular, even if the 'detachment' was no greater than a few feet. The earlier semi-detacheds were usually pebble-dashed plain square boxes with the slate roof of the nineteenth century, but by the Thirties they were mostly of brick and had roofs of red tiles. Terraced houses were still being built, but the romantic English ideas of privacy and a decent bit of garden all to yourself defeated the best intentions of the town planners. The most expensive semi-detacheds had a variety of features stuck on to give the much-desired air of individuality – bow windows and porches, a blossoming of turrets and latticed windows, even battlements. Many were miniature Tudor manors. In some streets no two were alike, so strong was the reaction against uniformity, and they had names instead of numbers. It was all in the old strong tradition of the English country house. Superior people mocked at these new houses but they were a great improvement on their predecessors, and the accusation that they were 'jerry-built' was untrue of the vast majority.

The revolutionary modern ideas of the great centre of architectural re-awakening in Germany, the Bauhaus, had not reached further than the intellectuals: architects preferred reinforced concrete but nobody else did and in fact the early concrete dwellings turned out to be a disappointment. The steel bars rusted and the rust leaked out through the concrete in orange and yellow streaks; besides, it was subject to a dark poison-green growth of algae, so that many early concrete dwellings looked highly macabre in a very short time, like something out of Edgar Allan Poe.

It was the era of the suburban tennis club and Mr Betjeman's adored 'Pam, you great big mountainous sports girl'. If your quite small income was reasonably secure, you could enjoy a very happy, active, highly organised and, of course, rather snobbish social life in the outer suburbs in the Thirties, with 'Who's for tennis?' as your watchword in the daytime and 'Shall we dance?' in the evenings, when the big sweet bands of Henry Hall and Jack Payne came flooding through on the wireless, and all was glamorous under the new electric light.

In the home the lighting was probably very new and might be 'indirect', being bounced off distempered walls to gleam on the 'fumed' or 'limed' oak furniture and draw a bluish flash from the chromium thing on the sideboard which looked like Isadora Duncan. But it was more likely to be directed downwards from a standard lamp. A feature of the Thirties, this was a light on top of a six-foot pole, with a heavy base. It bore an enormous shade like an

The entrance to one of the new housing estates being built in the suburbs. These houses are really good value for the money, and represent an enormous improvement, in human though not always in aesthetic terms, on the terraced houses of the past. *(Wates)*

The copper kettle culture, cosy, sentimental and warm. The galleon was, inexplicably, one of the most popular motifs of the age, and the stepped fireplace in porridge-coloured tiles disfigured thousands of homes. Most of the objects in this room are very much of the Thirties. Although completely unfashionable, they represent the taste of the majority. *(The Mansell Collection)*

umbrella in bright silk, with a long fringe at the edge. Though much mocked, it was very convenient since you could move your pool of light to any part of the room.

During the whole period between the wars, interior decoration and furnishings, like all the other arts, were in furious reaction against the Victorian belief in 'Nature'. I can remember a rather arty party in the early Thirties when a Victorian inkstand which had been made to represent a pomegranate surrounded by a wreath of silver daisies, an object which in these days would be considered quite charming, was greeted with loud expressions of nausea. Man's function in the Universe was seen as intellectual. Analysis was his job, not Nature worship. None of Nature's curves was acceptable any more, only segments of circles. Le Corbusier had decreed that a house should be 'a machine for living in' and a chair, therefore, by a logical extension, became 'a machine for sitting on'. In the Twenties, only those who were rich, leisured and intellectual enough to care pursued this ideal and they pursued it in its full rigour, but by the middle Thirties the idea of being 'modern' and 'bringing the house up to date' had percolated down to the middle of the middle class. The result was a softening of the austere ideal. A chair might be a machine for sitting on, but when you weren't sitting on it, you had to look at it. As women's curves returned, it began to be appreciated in the decorators' trade that Man, as well as being a machine for living, also had dreams, mostly of a sensual kind. But in the Tottenham Court Road, once the great effort of mental adjustment had been made and it was realised that 'if it was all angles it was all right', no further development followed and most decoration and furniture in the Thirties acknowledged that principle.

6 · *Politics*

Both Ramsay MacDonald and Stanley Baldwin who were jointly to rule over Great Britain with their National Government for most of the decade were mature Victorians, deeply embedded in the values of before-the-war. Sincere but backward-looking and complacent men, their instinct, when the Thirties storm began to blow, was to drop anchor and ride it out. Their achievement was that, when war broke out at the end of the period, the British faced it as one nation which they might well not have done if the extreme Right and Left had fought it out together: as it was, the centre held and Britain remained a social democracy, at the cost of being almost totally unprepared to face the war.

Ramsay MacDonald was a noble-looking creature, in the manner of some great Highland chieftain. Court dress well became him and he was fond of it. Originally the Labour Government had had some qualms about wearing court dress or even evening dress, remembering the lone cloth cap in the House of Commons of their first Labour Member, Keir Hardie. MacDonald never subscribed to these qualms and the higher he rose in social circles, the more he was in his element. In fact he was a snob; at one time so ardently did he frequent the soirees of Lady Londonderry, an upper-crust political hostess, that a member of the left wing of his own party, James Maxton, asked him in the House of Commons whether the Socialists' anthem was still 'The Red Flag' or had become 'The Londonderry Air'.

After his great decision to form a National Government, MacDonald rapidly became a spent force, and his speeches grew vaguer and vaguer: in one of them he proclaimed that the improvements wrought by Socialism would go 'on and on and on, and up and up and up', and that is precisely what he himself did until his feet were so far off the ground that he could deal only with huge generalisations and matters of principle.

Stanley Baldwin was a middle-class man, firmly based on the family's profitable iron-foundry in the Midlands. He was on one

Ramsay MacDonald, the leader of a party which had some qualms about the wearing of evening dress, himself revelled in the finery of office. It would have been tactless to show this picture of his assimilation into the Establishment in the depressed areas. *(Radio Times Hulton Picture Library)*

side of his nature a sort of minor Georgian poet, of the kind then being rent asunder by the Red intellectuals of Oxford. He had a genuine poet's passion for England, its countryside, its manners and customs and its literature. He was probably the most indolent Prime Minister that ever lived: he often spent his afternoons reading magazines in the House of Commons Library. Before becoming Prime Minister his standing had been quite undistinguished and it is on record that Mr Bonar Law, his predecessor as Conservative leader, had said during his last illness 'If I have to nominate my successor, I'm afraid it will have to be Baldwin'.

Baldwin hated the necessity of making decisions, and postponed or avoided these as much as possible, but once his mind was made up he was a tough operator, as devious and clever as a monkey: a hard-hitting speaker, too, when he was not lost in contemplation of his dream-England. But he had a fatal flaw which nearly cost this country its life: he preferred the second-rate. His own version of this preference was 'First-rate minds have second-rate characters'. It is not known if Mr Baldwin was the subject of Belloc's verse:

I knew a man who used to say,
Not once but twenty times a day,
That in 'The turmoil and the strife' –
His very phrase – of human life,
The thing of ultimate effect
Was character, not intellect.
He therefore was at constant pains
To atrophy his puny brains,
And registered success in this
Beyond the dreams of avarice.

but it suits Baldwin down to the ground, and even better the House of Commons of the time which, at least to the disaffected young, appeared to be a unique collection of zombies. At all events, not one of the really able and talented men of the time was ever called into the councils of the great.

Lloyd George, by far the ablest statesman then alive in Britain, was elbowed out in 1922 and not used again. Winston Churchill languished in the shadows throughout the Thirties, prophesying doom. Maynard Keynes, the Cambridge economist and a genius, was not co-opted in the crisis. Captain Liddell-Hart, the strategist and writer on military affairs, was publishing some new and very bright ideas about the use of armour in attack. Nobody in the Government or the War Office took any notice and we started the War about where Haig left off in 1918 – 'There'll always be a use for the horse, the well-bred horse' – only to find that the German Blitzkrieg, which drove us out through Dunkirk and won France for the Nazis, was largely of Liddell-Hart design. And Oswald Mosley . . .

Sir Oswald Mosley, sixth Baronet, stuck out like a sore thumb in the House of Commons. Not only was he young, handsome, brilliant, able and eloquent – all qualities in short supply there – but worse, he wanted action. He was a Conservative first, but could make no impact on those moss-grown ramparts so he joined the Labour Party, where he tried very hard to get J. H. Thomas, a useless Minister, to do something about the unemployed. Mosley had a quite sensible plan for increased allowances and organised public works, something like Roosevelt's New Deal, but the old men of the party didn't want to know about it. So he walked out in 1931 and formed a new party, taking with him some of the more dynamic men of the Left like John Strachey. But they soon left him when he bought himself a black shirt, raised a private army and took off down the right-hand road to Fascism. Soon his thugs were beating up Jews and marching through the East End of London on shop-wrecking expeditions.

There was not much the Labour Party could do since it was out in the cold after 1931. It polished up its propaganda and tried to formulate a clear-cut policy against MacDonaldism. For a time its leader was a highly Victorian figure, George Lansbury, a Christian Socialist of real integrity and piety. His line was that all would be solved when we had 'complete Socialism and power as well as office. Let's sing the "Red Flag" '. John Strachey wrote Marxist books and appeared to hover between Fascism and Communism. On the extreme Left, in the Independent Labour Party, a few revolutionary Socialists retained their seats. The most picturesque was James Maxton, whose black hair fell across one of his burning eyes and reached his shoulder. His narrow, pale, emaciated face would have served any romantic painter for a picture called 'To the Barricades'. Throughout the crisis years the House of Commons remained 'the best club in London'.

Politics were not so cosy abroad. In Germany a failed art student, whose painting bore no trace of the contemporary ferment, was rising in the world. While we could think of nothing to do about our three million unemployed, Adolf Hitler had great plans for Germany's six million.

Germany's history since the War had been appalling. The Allies had kept up the blockade until the Treaty of Versailles had been signed, and that had meant starvation in Germany. Many children had died and very many more were crippled with deficiency diseases such as rickets. This was neither forgiven nor forgotten. The Treaty itself was guaranteed to sow hatred everywhere and to paralyse Germany. The reparations demanded were impossible to fulfil: a grotesque inflation of the currency followed and at one time the German mark was quoted at fifteen million to the pound sterling. The French and the Belgians marched in and occupied the main industrial belt, the Ruhr, to enforce their demands.

It was at this low ebb in Germany's fortunes that Hitler launched his first abortive putsch with General Ludendorff. When it failed, Hitler was sentenced to five years in prison, most of which he didn't serve; but he occupied his time in gaol by writing his manifesto *Mein Kampf* which plainly showed the trend of his mind and his imperialistic intentions: nobody over here took them seriously. German insolvency in the Twenties and the depression which now set in in the Thirties had brought the country to the verge of revolution. Nobody would have been surprised if Ger-

George Lansbury (with the white whiskers) visiting a Jewish school in the East End of London. Lansbury, a sincere Christian Socialist, was for a time the leader of the orthodox Labour Party after its defeat by the National Government. He made great efforts to improve the conditions of life of the children of the London poor. *(Radio Times Hulton Picture Library)*

many had gone Communist by a sudden coup, and the German middle classes had long trembled on the brink of disaster. It took them some time to realise that the title of Hitler's party, the National Socialist Party, was extremely misleading, that what he stood for was paranoid nationalism, racialism and militarism, with the Jews as internal scapegoats; but when they did, they began to see him as the saviour who would discipline the working class, rid the business men of their smarter competitors, the Jews, and make the name of Germany feared once more in the world. The aristocratic land-owning class, the Junkers, saw in him a useful weapon against Communism: the unemployed were in a mood for a saviour of some sort and democracy was a very new and foreign growth in Germany. They were used to dictatorial masters: now they were all going to be masters – the Master Race, which they had always known in their hearts that they were. Bankers now began to see the point of keeping him in funds.

The Weimar Republic of Germany, which Hitler was to take over in 1933, was the pet of the intelligentsia, the first tolerant and permissive society in Europe, teeming with liberal good intention, particularly kind to sexual deviants who flocked there from all over the place. But the lost war rankled in the hearts of many old soldiers still in their thirties, who had fallen for the lie that the

Coal queues like this had been commonplace in Germany since before the end of the war. The woman on the right has brought a sledge to drag a bag of coal back through the streets. On the dissatisfactions bred in this kind of group, Hitler was borne to power. *(Radio Times Hulton Picture Library)*

German Army was never defeated and that panic among the civilians had dictated the surrender. They could be made to see the Weimar Republic as something soft, decadent and shameful, particularly if they were unemployed. Hitler, who in the Twenties had been a loud mouth in a beer cellar, was by now something to be reckoned with.

He was soon to be seen with the better-dressed agents of Germany's downfall, like Von Papen. President Hindenburg's idea was to let Hitler loose on the Communists and then stamp on Hitler. Unfortunately it didn't work out that way. Hitler reached absolute power in 1933. It was Hindenburg that died and with him the old Germany he stood for.

How did it come about that the Germans, with their most liberal republic, and the most powerful Communist party outside Russia, came to be saddled with Hitler? Let me quote John Manders, from his book *Berlin—The Eagle and The Bear*:

> For a time the extreme Left and the extreme Right seemed to be running neck and neck. But Communism had a fatal handicap; its revolution had already taken place, and the German people had been able to observe it at fairly close range. The German people were sick of the class struggle, sick of capitalism, sick of the Jews, sick of democracy, and above all, sick of Berlin, that modern Gomorrah and the source of all their ills. There is no great mystery about Hitler's coming to power. The simplest explanation is the best: the German people chose him.

7 · *Marching in Step*

The sight of the unemployed marching, usually with banners to draw attention to their plight, was nothing new – there had been a march of the unemployed in 1920. In the Twenties marchers usually wore their medals or some scrap of Army uniform to drive home the message that they had served their country and been thrown on the scrapheap, but now the War was too far away to be relevant and marchers marched to gain sympathy, to show the well-fed the true state of the nation (which got a poor showing in the Press), and to force authority to get off its fat bottom and do something – particularly about the means test. They never achieved anything and may well have reinforced the close-knit solidarity of the better-off in leaving them to their fate, since a column of marching men is the classic threat of force, people felt insecure and town clerks all over the country were remarkably ready with the Riot Act.

The great marches began in the Thirties. In 1931, 2,500 unemployed marched on London and were met by a baton charge of police in Hyde Park, and broken up. It was a very rough occasion. They had deposited an enormous petition which they hoped to present to Parliament in the left luggage office at a London terminus. When they went to pick it up, it had 'unaccountably' disappeared and so was never presented. In 1934 there was another march of the same kind which reached the House of Commons without a struggle, but failed to flush out Ramsay MacDonald, the Prime Minister, to receive a delegation.

But the march to end all marches was the Jarrow March of 1936. Of all the black, noxious, stinking industrial hell-holes left behind by nineteenth century enterprise, the town of Jarrow was just about the nethermost pit. In the history books, on the other hand, its name smells very sweetly, for it was here that the Venerable Bede in the seventh century kept the flame of civilisation alive when all Europe was sunk in barbarism. Thereafter Jarrow slept in the odour of sanctity until the eighteenth century, when it became a mining village. In 1852 Palmers Shipyard arrived and transformed it. A visitor in 1876 found a clergyman friend of his 'amongst a teeming population of blackened, foulmouthed, drunken rogues, living in rows of dismal houses in a country where every vestige of vegetation is killed by noxious chemical vapours, on the edge of a slimy marsh, with a distant inky sky, and the furnaces vomiting forth volumes of blackened smoke. All nature seemed parched and writhing under the pollution.' Jarrow's population had risen to 35,000 in the Twenties, and now in the Thirties a firm called National Shipbuilding Security Ltd, whose speciality was buying up enterprises hit by the slump, moved into Jarrow and dismantled Palmers Yard. It had a powerful ally in Walter Runciman at the Board of Trade.

Jarrow depended entirely on shipbuilding for its living. With its shipyard shut, the sky cleared, the river ran clear again, birds sang and silence reigned and such a blight descended on the town as to make its previous squalor and savagery seem a memory of paradise. Jarrow was dead.

Jarrow's response was to behave like one stricken family singled out for misfortune. Internal bickerings and differences were

This photograph was taken after the police baton charge which broke up the 1931 march of unemployed in Hyde Park. Several hundred of the marchers are fed from a food wagon. In the circumstances, the crowd looks surprisingly calm and orderly. *(Radio Times Hulton Picture Library)*

packed away, as in a war, 'for the duration of the emergency'. Everybody did what he could to help but when, in response to delegations, Runciman's final answer was delivered – 'Jarrow must work out its own salvation' – they knew they were on their own. They decided on a great crusade.

The Member of Parliament, Ellen Wilkinson, was the moving spirit in Jarrow; a small, slight, red-haired ball of fire, the year before she had led a march in a great storm to beard Ramsay MacDonald in his constituency of Seaham, fifteen miles away. In the event, all that march achieved was a bleating admonition from the cornered statesman: 'Ellen, why don't you go out and preach Socialism, which is the only remedy for all this?'

And so, on 5 October, two hundred picked men set out under a banner 'Jarrow Crusade' to march to London, about three hundred miles away, as an official delegation to Parliament. Everybody turned out to watch them go. The Mayor and Mayoress led them for the first twelve miles and, after that, Ellen Wilkinson.

On the whole, the marchers were well received. The Press, with only a few dissentients, was greatly in their favour. They were royally treated in some of the towns they passed through. In

Ellen Wilkinson MP, the fiery particle, was a moving spirit in the organisation of the march and headed the column most of the way. The Jarrow march made a strong impact on popular feeling, but achieved absolutely no solid results. *(Radio Times Hulton Picture Library)*

Leicester the Co-op worked all night mending their boots. Bedford, in the suspect South, rallied to their support. As they drew near London a thousand Blackshirts were parading through Bethnal Green. They came into London in a cloudburst with their mouth-organ band playing 'The Minstrel Boy', but as they marched through the West End which bore no trace of hard times and seemed utterly indifferent they felt alien. In the House of Commons Gallery they heard their MP deliver the petition and speak of their plight. They heard Walter Runciman, who had the nerve to say that his information was that the situation in Jarrow was improving, refuse to answer a question about them because it was not on the Order Paper; saw Mr Baldwin, the Prime Minister, refuse to say anything – and that was it.

They went home by train and had their dole cut because they had not been 'available for work', though none had been offered. Ellen Wilkinson was rebuked at a Labour Party Conference for her 'irresponsibility' and the whole chapter was closed.

Jarrow was the classic march, but even while it was going on, other marches were in progress. Four hundred Scotsmen from Glasgow, for instance, were marching south to join up with other contingents. Marching became an epidemic in the Thirties and not only in Britain.

Mosley's Fascists took full advantage of the general restlessness and stepped up their parades until the East End was being invaded almost every night. They had no doctrines except jingoism, a professed love of the British flag and the Royal Family and a hatred of Jews and Communists. They always marched with a heavy guard of police, who seemed to be as much part of their parade as their own 'biff boys'. At Mosley meetings the formula was usually the same. When the hall was filled the doors were locked and the speeches began. There was a spotlight worked from the platform and if any heckler interrupted, or even if anyone rose from his seat, he would be caught in the spotlight and as he stood there blinded and helpless a squad of 'biff boys' would move in on him and give him a savage beating up in view of the audience, before turning him out of the hall.

It was an age addicted to psychological explanations, but I never

Overleaf

May Day was traditionally a Socialist festival. Here in Bermondsey in 1938 the Fascists hold a counter-rally. The Facist salute, taken very seriously by the party, was regarded as richly comic by most of the public. The East End, with its large Jewish population, was the chief battleground of the opposing factions. *(Radio Times Hulton Picture Library)*

heard the nature of Mosley's audiences satisfactorily explained. Who were these people who submitted themselves night after night to this exhibition of terrorism and tyranny? They looked middle-aged on the whole and seemed to be enveloped in general and political apathy, yet they kept on coming. Mosley was never short of an audience.

The Communists and the Fascists met and fought from time to time, but the habit never became a public menace as it was in Berlin in the early Thirties when it was extremely easy for anybody, particularly at night, to be caught up in some skirmish between Nazis and Communists and be beaten up or, quite often, never heard of again.

On the Continent, marching was very different: it had become a passion. The chief ally of the dictators – and Mussolini had been Dictator in Italy since 1922 – was the drill sergeant and all over Germany and Italy, and in Russia, armies of young men now took pride in immaculately correct mass movements, both of body and mind, and the full rigour of discipline.

There had been 'Youth' movements in Germany in the nineteenth century and the best known of them, the Wandervogel, were very much in vogue in the Twenties. They were groups of young men and women – but often of young men only, for there was a vague homosexual flavour about the movement – who walked in the open air over long distances, often for weeks at a time, and sang romantic lieder around the campfires at night to the accompaniment of beribboned mandolins (the guitar was still strictly a Latin instrument).

I went for a wander with the Wandervogel once in the late Twenties. This was a mixed group and my companion was a boundlessly silly girl called Eva with flaxen hair wound round her head in plaits. She had set up as a sort of priestess of the Goddess of Nature; her brother Ernst, who was well-named, was a pacifist and an anarchist and drunk on the poems of Heine and the songs of Schubert. He was a Wordworthian young man. There was plenty of silly talk about the Aryans, but it was romantic, not aggressive. The main theme was the necessity for opting out from under the frightful old men who had made the last war and detested freedom everywhere.

By the early Thirties the Nazi Youth Leader, Baldur von Schirach, had funnelled all these fledgelings into the Hitler Jugend. I met Ernst and some of his companions in 1936 between their bouts of square-bashing and what a change had been wrought in these romantic, rather humourless, but likeable youths! They had become arrogant in a petulant way: every sentence began with 'Of course', followed by some bloody-minded paradox; 'Of course we must separate ourselves from the Jews: it is the way to true community'; 'Of course we want peace, and we shall give it to you whether you want it or not'. Their great word was 'decadent': anything which showed the least sign of liberalism, tolerance or even civilisation was 'dekadent'.

This infection of mass conditioning did cross the Channel, but the virus bred much milder mutations in the British atmosphere. Community singing was one. In the Thirties, crowds at football matches or at political meetings, or waiting to watch some state occasion, or quite often simply convened for the purpose, burst into community song under some self-appointed conductor. Their repertoire consisted mainly of hymn tunes of the more depressing sort; 'Abide with Me' was the favourite. Certainly the 'Eventide' was fast falling but they, as it happened, were the last to know that.

The Women's League of Health and Beauty, led by Prunella Stack, was another of its manifestations. Under her guidance, groups of women in every town and village in the land disported

Something of the Germanic enthusiasm for drill percolated into Britain during the decade. Such organisations as the Women's League of Health and Beauty gave public demonstrations of physical fitness and had an enormous membership all over the country. *(Women's League of Health and Beauty)*

themselves in orgies of physical training, rolling about on the floors of gymnasiums, drill halls and village institutes, clad in a uniform of shorts and white satin blouses.

'Hiking' began early in the Thirties. 'Going for walks' through the countryside had been an English pastime for centuries; in the Thirties the countryside was much more attractive than it is now for two main reasons: agricultural workers, unable to live on their wages during the Depression, had moved in large numbers to the towns, so fields were ill-tended and wild plants grew everywhere. Every field had a wide verge where wild flowers grew in sheets and clumps and the verges of the country roads were the same. Chemical sprays had not yet arrived to achieve that dull uniformity of efficient farming which is ubiquitous today.

Walking became a mass pursuit, with a uniform to mark the fact. In shorts and open shirts and carrying huge rucksacks on their backs, they invaded the countryside in vast numbers. Special trains ran from the big cities to take them out to the wilder spots. Sometimes they hiked in hundreds, sometimes in dozens: more usually in fives and sixes. The body, which had meant sex in the Twenties, now meant health and hygiene. Sunbathing and nudism were also pursuits which, for some reason, had to be done in groups. These were derived from nature therapies devised by the Germans to help children who suffered from malnutrition in the days of the Allied blockade and starvation.

Towards the end of the decade, the intelligentsia became obsessed with the collection of facts. Documentary film flourished and one of the great names was Paul Rotha. Tom Harrisson, a young anthropologist, and Charles Madge, the poet, invented 'mass observation'. The 'mass observer', with pencil and notebook, was everywhere: he would join a dole queue to find out what, if anything, was said in those sad processions. He would sit in the midst of holidaymakers at the seaside and take down their conversations. He would record the graffiti in railway station lavatories or the tea-time small talk at a diocesan conference. Undergraduates joined in and began to write poems in groups. A famous group based on religious feeling was the 'Buchmanites', founded by an American, John Buchman. These called themselves the 'Oxford Group', but had no real right to the title. They believed in group confession, clean living (ie no sex) and general goodwill. They were well-washed, well-shaved, antiseptic sort of people; well-heeled, too, but not the sort to set the soul aflame: their most notable convert was the famous tennis-player, Bunny Austin. But, on the whole, the ravages of mass conditioning were very slight in Britain. In spite of Mosley's Blackshirts and the Communists, true mass thinking and feeling on the Continental model never arrived and the British, except in matters of class observances, remained undocile to the end of the decade.

Hikers, in their own peculiar uniform of shorts, shirts and rucksacks, were to be seen at all the London railway stations, taking off for a day's march in the country. They often moved in groups of twenty or thirty at a time and were organised into clubs for the purpose. *(Radio Times Hulton Picture Library)*

8 · *Entertainment*

In an age like ours, when so many people have given up having lives to have a television instead, it is difficult to imagine what ordinary family entertainment consisted of before there was a box to look at. It is true that most families were grouped around a wireless set in the evenings, but the wireless in the Thirties was not at all the same thing. Television does your imagining for you: the wireless excited your own imagination and, since it was largely verbal, tended to reinforce the older culture of reading. If, in a way, it was less satisfying than television, it was far more stimulating and Sir John Reith made sure that the diet, though somewhat austere and puritanical, was of good quality.

In the Twenties the wireless had been a cross between a scientific toy and a miracle which would one day unite the nations. By the Thirties the miracle was taken for granted, except when the King broadcast to the Empire on Christmas Day. On these great occasions, which began in 1932, the hour-long programme of Empire messages of cheer and goodwill from every quarter of the globe (professionally known as the 'round-the-world-hook-up') which preceded the King's talk brought back all the old sense of wonder.

By the Thirties the BBC had lost its rather hearty amateur sense of fun and become highly professional. Great strides had been made in the techniques of outside broadcasting: the voices of Howard Marshall and John Snagge were seldom off the air, from the Oxford and Cambridge Boat Race in early spring to the end of the cricket season. London was, in those days, self-consciously an Imperial city and the BBC became a masterly impresario of great state occasions, the first of which was the wedding in 1934 of Prince George, the Duke of Kent, to Princess Marina of Greece, who was to be the leader of British fashion during the Thirties: she gave her name to a hairstyle which became a craze and her hats were instantly copied for the shops in the High Street.

The speciality of the time was nostalgic music. Eric

Maschwitz's *Goodnight Vienna*, later made into a film starring Anna Neagle, was a characteristic show and later his *Balalaika* was another popular radio hit. The real Europe having returned to barbarism, it seemed best to remember it as Ruritania. Noel Coward's *Bittersweet* was broadcast in 1935 to coincide with King George's Silver Jubilee.

The BBC Symphony Orchestra, with its 114 players under their permanent conductor Adrian Boult, made its debut in 1930 at the Queen's Hall and in 1933 there was a technical revolution when the terrible old steel-tape recorder, the Blattnerphone, was superseded by disc recording; in 1935 disc-cutting machines were installed in cars and the 'Mobile Recording Unit' began. This was of immense significance, particularly to the compilers of programmes like Leslie Baily's *Scrapbooks*, in each of which a particular year was recalled by voice, sound and music, or *In Town Tonight*, in which a mighty shout of 'Stop!' cut short 'the roar of London's traffic' to introduce items of London life from that par-

All the stops were pulled out for the wedding of Prince George of Kent to Princess Marina of Greece. The bride was young, elegant and relatively poor, and the match had the elements of a Cinderella story. She became extremely popular, particularly among the working girls of the country, who looked to her as a leader of fashion. *(Keystone Press Agency Ltd)*

ticular week. Both these programmes had enormous audiences, and went on for many years.

Wireless comedians included some who had already made their reputations in the Twenties, like Mabel Constanduros with her sketches about 'Grandma', and John Henry complaining of his wife 'Blossom'. Famous in the Thirties were Arthur Askey (Bighearted Arthur) who is still playing, Richard (Stinker) Murdoch, Clapham and Dwyer, Ronald Frankau 'the only conscious comedian from Eton' with his famous song 'I'd rather be an Ethiopian savage than an ordinary civilized man', and the Western Brothers, monocled and suave. Reginald Foort presided at the mighty organ until, at the end of the decade, he handed it over to Sandy MacPherson, who played us through the Phoney War and into action. For many people the BBC was synonymous with Christopher Stone and his programme of gramophone records. Impossible to analyse his charm or give any explanation of why millions of people made his programme of (mostly) romantic music the great date of their week. Lastly, another 'natural', the gardening expert, never referred to in any other way but as 'Mr Middleton'.

It must be said that Sir John Reith's influence on Sunday broadcasting was dire and millions tuned out the BBC and in to Radio Luxembourg, from which a stream of popular gramophone music interspersed with advertising jingles flowed across the North Sea on Sunday mornings. One of these jingles 'We are the Ovalteenies' became a popular hit.

For me, the voices of the Thirties are John Snagge, the deep, slow, unpompous voice of the Thirties BBC, Richard Tauber endlessly singing 'You are my heart's delight', Flanagan and Allen with 'Underneath the arches, I dream my dreams away', Gracie Fields, unbelievably British, with her powerful soprano from Lancashire, on top of which she could add another octave in a piercing falsetto for rendering such ditties as 'Walter, Walter, lead me to the altar', and anybody's voice who happens to be singing

The smile of Garbo and the scent of roses,
The waiters whistling as the last bar closes,
That song that Crosby sings,
These foolish things remind me of you.

They were all on 'the wireless'.

Radio had been the miracle of the Twenties: the new miracle was the 'talkies'. They had arrived in 1928 but for the first few years were so busy demonstrating the great new magic that sound, in huge quantities, could be married to film, that as films they were greatly inferior to the old silent movies. When they recovered their poise they were 'all talking, all singing, all dancing', and all through the decade there was a constant flow of giant American musical spectaculars with casts of hundreds of delicious girls in feathers, their prancings even better drilled than the Nazis, with sweet warm music at about two hundred decibels. When the cast included Fred Astaire and Ginger Rogers and, say, Cole Porter had written the songs, these super-productions were splendid entertainment.

Many of the old silent stars did not survive the change to talkies because their voices were unusable but to some, like Greta Garbo, it was a happy release not to have to make the point so powerfully with grimace and gesture: her delicate art of understatement flowered with the new techniques. The British did well out of it, too, now that it was possible for a film actor to be to some extent less obvious and to use the arts he had learnt for the stage. Herbert

The piano player is Henry Hall, the leader of the BBC Dance Band and one of the great names in entertainment throughout the Thirties. Gracie Fields and George Formby, both Northeners in the old Music Hall tradition, were stage, radio and film stars of the first magnitude. *(Keystone Press Agency Ltd)*

Marshall, Robert Donat, Clive Brook and Leslie Howard were yearned over by millions. People did not exactly yearn over Charles Laughton, but they flocked to see him. Chaplin's silent film *City Lights* made five million dollars but when it comes into your mind you do not immediately think of the Thirties, as you do whenever Mae West pops up ('Come up and see me sometime'), or Gary Cooper in *Mr Deeds Comes to Town*, or Wendy Hillier and Leslie Howard in *Pygmalion*. In Britain, the favourite stars in their order as moneymakers were Shirley Temple a millionaire at the age of nine, Clark Gable, Gracie Fields, Gary Cooper, George Formby, William Powell, Jeanette MacDonald, Robert Taylor, Fred Astaire and Ginger Rogers and Laurel and Hardy.

In spite of the sweet romanticism prevailing in the film industry,

A by-product of the Hollywood boom was the film magazine. Cheap and lavishly illustrated, these 'mags' made the private lives of the stars – or what were alleged to be their private lives – into public property. Ronald Colman was a sure-fire heart-throb, and his little moustache became a cult.

Left.
Astaire's partnership with Ginger Rogers in films like *Top Hat* raised the standards of film musicals for his own day and thereafter. There was a time, during the middle Thirties, when practically everyone in Britain seemed to be whistling 'Cheek to Cheek'. *(National Film Archive)*

there was a strong anti-sentimental lobby in the Thirties, and the Marx Brothers' comedy, divorced altogether from pathos or even pity, was highly characteristic of the decade's sophisticated outlook. But Laurel and Hardy's more fully human choice of viewpoint still filled the cinemas and Chaplin simply took the revolution in his stride. Walt Disney's arkful of comic animals were of the Thirties too, though Mickey Mouse had arrived in 1929. *Snow White*, Disney's first full-length cartoon feature, was released in 1938 when the Thirties show was nearly over. Noble sentiment was supplied by the dog hero, Rin-Tin-Tin, always to the rescue, and the young Judy Garland moved those who found Miss Temple's performance of 'The good ship Lollipop' a trifle over-sticky. Perhaps Bing Crosby's triumph was the most complete: everybody liked Bing Crosby.

The cinema in the Thirties was more than an entertainment: it was a retreat, almost a shrine. Some of the super-cinemas could accommodate three thousand people. Sixpence would buy three hours of blissful escape from the harsh squalor of the real world. There was warmth and privacy, unattainable at home for at least one third of the people of Britain: there was a soft seat in ultra-plutocratic surroundings, and besides the cheap and easy dream devised for you by Hollywood to 'take you out of yourself', there was a rich syrup of music supplied by the organ – the 'Mighty Wurlitzer' – which from time to time rose from the depths like a submarine and filled you right up to the top with Ketelbey's 'In a Monastery Garden' or some similar fantasy of blessing and stability before submerging once more into the basement. 'Going to the pictures' was a favourite form of family outing. You didn't go to see any particular film, except that you avoided the sort of films you didn't care for. You could have a large tea in the 'tea lounge' off the circle or, more likely, buy a bar of chocolate or a bag of sweets in the foyer. Late in the decade a new invention, 'choc ices', were available in the interval. Saturday mornings were reserved, in the smaller cinemas, for the children. For a copper or two they could riot there for hours on a diet of Westerns and Disney. The sound of their appreciation was often audible several streets away.

For nearly everybody, the cinema was the anaesthetic of the age. Even the newsreels formalised and subtly improved upon reality, a point made by Cecil Day Lewis in this poem, 'Newsreel':

> Enter the dream-house, brothers and sisters, leaving
> Your debts asleep, your history at the door:

This is the home for heroes, and this loving
Darkness a fur you can afford.

Fish in their tank electrically heated
Nose without envy the glass wall: for them
Clerk, spy, nurse, killer, prince, the great and the defeated,
Move in a mute day-dream.

Bathed in this common source, you gape incurious
At what your active hours have willed –
Sleep-walking on that silver wall, the furious
Sick shapes and pregnant fancies of your world.

There is the mayor opening the oyster season:
A society wedding: the autumn hats look swell:
An old crocks' race, and a politician
In fishing-waders to prove that all is well.

Oh, look at the warplanes! Screaming hysteric treble
In the long power-dive, like gannets they fall steep.
But what are they to trouble –
These silver shadows to trouble your watery, womb-deep
sleep?

See the big guns, rising, groping, erected
To plant death in your world's soft womb.
Fire-bud, smoke-blossom, iron seed projected –
Are these exotics? They will grow nearer home:

Grow nearer home – and out of the dream-house stumbling
One night into a strangling air and the flung
Rags of children and thunder of stone niagaras tumbling,
You'll know you slept too long.

Outside in the sunshine, if you could forget about the unemployed, Britain exhibited a fine growth of democracy. The roads to the seaside were jammed with family cars and swimming pools were crowded. Thousands of people had tasted the delights of flying in Alan Cobham's Air Circuses. In spite of the dramatic achievements in that field during the Twenties when the 'conquests of the air' provided some new sensation every few months, flying was still glamorous. Amy Johnson proved it. Lindberg's flight from America to Paris in the Twenties had put him on a pedestal labelled 'All-American Boy'. The one marked 'Truly British Girl' was claimed by Amy. She was a pretty girl, brought up in Hull where her father owned a fish business, and flying for her was an escape from the humdrum into the high altitude where popular heroes lived. She was a solicitor's typist but had made herself a fully qualified pilot and mechanic, a rare combination. She wrote to Sir Sefton Branker, the Civil Aviation Chief, about her ambition and Sir Sefton found sponsors for her. Amy bought an old green Gipsy Moth, called it Jason, rebuilt it with her own hands and flew single-handed to Australia in it in 1930. She was an instant success. She was 'our' Amy much as Gracie Fields, the Lancashire mill-girl singer, was 'our Gracie'. But that was not because of any warm proletarian solidarity on Amy's part, but merely the result of a Yorkshire accent. Amy herself filled the role of popular heroine and played the part of the wonder-girl faultlessly for years. She married Jim Mollison, another record-breaking flyer in the newspaper headlines. For some time they

The young Amy Johnson in her old green Gipsy Moth called Jason, just before she set off on her single-handed flight to Australia in 1930. She had rebuilt the plane with her own hands. Note the spare propeller roped to the struts. *(Keystone Press Agency Ltd)*

were the pets of the Press – 'first husband and wife to fly the Atlantic' – but Mollison was something of a playboy and not really as good a flyer as Amy. When they were divorced the Press was greatly enraged, though it had had more than its money's worth out of them. The Amy Johnson serial died with the decade and she crashed, unpublicised, during the War while patriotically flying a transport plane.

Heroes and heroines were much sought after in the Thirties and particularly the heroes of sport. Thousands crammed the stands at Wimbledon where our own Bunny Austin and Betty Nuthall fought bravely and long against the great Americans, but never quite made it. Soccer was, as always, the basic British game with its fans to be counted in millions. But it was a proletarian game and being also a professional game it had little prestige at the time – professional was a dirty word. The professionals were ill-paid and it is impossible to determine whether the standard of play was anything like it now is. Stanley Matthews was the great football idol, famous not only for the quality of his technique but for his impeccable sportsmanship. In a career spanning in all thirty-three years he never received a caution on the field, and when in 1938 there was a rumour that he might be leaving Stoke City, there was a near-riot by fans pleading that he should stay. The Monarch regularly watched the Cup Final at Wembley, and by 1936 the increase in interest in Association football had another by-product: five and a half million people were entering their weekly coupons for the Pools.

But, for all that, soccer was never an Empire game while cricket was that – and more: it was part of the culture of England and combined enormous prestige with wide popularity. Cricket retained its full snobbishness in the Thirties and this was part of its appeal. There was a Gentlemen v Players match which nobody thought at all odd and amateurs were given their full panoply of initials on the scoreboard and in the newspapers – J. W. H. T. Douglas, for example, or A. P. F. Chapman, while the great Jack Hobbs, who retired in 1934 with 61,221 runs to his credit in a career of 29 years, was just Hobbs. And cricket was morally as well as socially significant. To schoolmasters and clergymen, the 'straight bat' was not altogether of this world, but had a heavenly counterpart, not overlooked by the 'Great Umpire'.

In 1933, the year that Hitler came to power, cricket shook the Empire and nearly provoked a diplomatic incident. This was the 'bodyline bowling' row or, as the English preferred to call it 'leg theory'. The problem which 'leg theory' set out to solve was how to get Bradman out. Don Bradman first appeared in this country, a member of the Australian touring side, in 1930. He played with faultless ease like a machine, scoring double centuries and treble centuries, a rock-like menace to England's hopes for the 1932-3 Australian Tour. The 'leg theory' dreamed up between the English captain D. R. Jardine and the fast bowler Larwood was simply this: if you bowl very fast, always on the leg side and with plenty of bouncers, and place a thick hedge of fielders on the same side, Bradman will in the end be caught out. Put into practice at Adelaide, 'leg theory' had all the appearance of attempted murder. As the injured staggered from the ground, Oldfield with a knock on the head which cracked his skull and Woodfull from a blow over the heart which hit him 'with a thud that was heard in the grandstand', the Australian crowd began to barrack and bay for blood and, halfway through the match, the Australian Board of Cricket Control sent a cable to the MCC in which they used the word 'unsportsmanlike'. All England was aghast. But then the MCC produced a stroke of diplomatic brinkmanship. In their reply they deplored the word 'unsportsmanlike', but said that if the Australians wanted to bring the tour to a close they would 'with great reluctance' consent. The tour continued. It was a shameful spectacle and the next time the Australians toured England, Larwood and Voce, the other fast bowler, were both dropped from the English side. Technically, though, 'leg theory' had worked: at Adelaide Bradman was out for 34.

The world heavyweight boxing title created much more sensation than it now does, though its greatest days were in the Twenties before the depression. It was normal for the champion to be an American, but there were three successful European contenders during the period, two Germans, Max Schmelling (1930) and Max Baer (1934), and one Italian, the gigantic Primo Carnera, known as the Ambling Alp, in 1933. The status quo was restored by the great Joe Louis, the Brown Bomber, in 1937. Louis retired undefeated in 1949 and was responsible, almost singlehanded, for the fading out of the colour bar and the acceptance of the negro in American sport.

In 1936 it was the turn of Berlin to act as host at the Olympic Games. Hitler naturally turned the occasion into a Nordic spectacular of Aryan superiority and the will to win of the Master Race. It was a great blow to him when most of the honours were carried off by the Americans, and a quite disproportionate number of them by American negroes, above all by Jesse Owens, who won four gold medals and broke two world records. Hitler refused to present his medals, and was popularly supposed to have rolled on the floor in his fury.

The Triple Crown, the world speed record for land, sea and air, was a prize greatly envied by the nations. Sir Henry Segrave, a popular hero, won the land record in 1929 at 231mph in his car 'Golden Arrow'. In 1931 he took his speedboat 'Miss England II' to Windermere for an attempt on the water record, and on Friday 13 June he was killed when his boat hit some flotsam on the water and sank. He was thrown clear, and lived just long enough to know he had broken the record. In 1932 Britain won the air contest, the Schneider Trophy, for good. Sir Malcolm Campbell, who had been neck and neck with Segrave since 1923, increased the world land speed record to 301.129mph in 1935, and the water speed record to 129.91mph in 1937. Both men were national heroes.

National rivalries were front page news on the tennis courts, too. Britain's great year was 1933, when we won the Davis Cup against competition from 32 other countries. The British star was

Jesse Owens, the American athlete who, at the Olympic Games in 1936 which were held in Berlin, upset all Hitler's plans to make the Games an advertisement for the superiority of the Nordic Race in general and the Germans in particular. Owens won four gold medals and broke two world records. Hitler, it was said at the time, rolled on the floor in his fury. *(National Film Archive)*

undoubtedly Fred Perry, who won at Wimbledon for three successive years from 1934, and at Forest Hills in 1933, '34 and '36. With 'Bunny' Austin, he held the sporting headlines until displaced by the American, Budge, towards the end of the decade. The women's matches were dominated by two Californian girls, Helen Wills and Alice Marble.

In golf, too, the Americans ruled the roost with players like Bobby Jones, Gene Sarazen and Walter Hagen; but T. H. Cotton, the finest British player of his time, gave them a run for their money and won the British Open Championship in 1934 and 1937.

The sunbathing cult came to its full flower at about the turn of the decade. The two-piece swimsuit had not yet arrived and most of them still had little skirts, but in response to fashion's peremptory demands for large areas of sunburned skin, openings were sculpted into these garments, exposing the ribs. Women's costumes became backless and this last alteration spread to evening dress, so that the suntan could be exhibited at leisure; during much of the Thirties, therefore, whether bathing or dining or dancing, women from the rear view were naked to the waist.

One result of the Wall Street crash in 1929 was that Americans could no longer afford to travel and the British shipping companies had to fill the gap, so cheap cruises to the Mediterranean and the Baltic began, with dances, fancy dress competitions, deck sports, swimming races and picture shows. People wore really colourful clothes on these trips, and this may have hastened a general brightening of the British scene, where the almost universal browns and greys and navy blues of men's ordinary clothes were gradually giving way to brighter colours. Starched collars and shirt fronts with dinner jackets swiftly became old-fashioned, and suede shoes arrived. In 1931, according to the *Daily Express*, 1,500 lipsticks were sold in London shops for every one sold ten years before. Nail varnish – often in mad shades – came in: there were blue nails and black nails, orange lipsticks and green eye sockets.

London seemed, and was – at least in the West End even during the depression – fabulously wealthy. Fashionable restaurants were redecorated at enormous cost every two years or so. The night club, the cocktail bar and the cabaret, inventions of the Twenties, increased their custom in the Thirties. A good barman had a repertoire of at least a dozen different cocktails to be made on demand.

But all this was for the few. For most people perhaps the chief source of entertainment amongst the literate in the Thirties was reading. It was a great decade for books and writers, and readers were very well served: besides the normal free libraries there were many others where, for some small sum ranging from a penny to sixpence, you could borrow a book for a fortnight. Boots the Chemists ran a library at most branches and travelling libraries toured the villages. The thriller had given place to the detective story and Agatha Christie and Dorothy Sayers kept us well supplied with literate mysteries with upper-middle-class settings and enough clues to give the intelligent reader just a chance of solving the problem before the last chapter. A nationwide controversy broke out over one of Agatha Christie's books *The Murder of Roger Ackroyd* because, it was alleged, no reader could have solved the problem. The book is written in the first person by the village doctor and at one point he says 'I did what had to be done', and what had to be done turned out in the end to be, not the examination of the corpse, but the murder. Was this a fair clue? Thousands of people became very heated over this question.

Graham Greene began his career in the Thirties, and gave us some good examples of the kind of books he preferred to call 'entertainments': his serious masterpiece *Brighton Rock* was published in 1938.

Aldous Huxley was perhaps the most characteristically Thirties phenomenon among the writers. Clinical and cool and consumed with curiosity, he had read enormously and always carried about with him on his travels an India-paper set of the *Encyclopaedia Britannica*. In the sense that a 'writer' is deeply in the soup with the rest of us, he was not really a writer at all but a polymath, observing the human race from the intellectual stratosphere and trying hard to overcome the disadvantages of this position. His book *Brave New World* in 1932 was really about trends and marked out a line between the past and what seemed likely to be the future – in his view, the difference between the religious outlook and scientific mass-conditioning. He was the middle classes' guide to sophistication. He was at one time a guide through the world of dark, instinctive drives and primitive percepts in which D. H. Lawrence had his being, and then he explored the world of psychedelic drugs like mescalin and became the guide through that. During the Thirties he was the chief representative of the enquiring mind.

T. S. Eliot, still in his forties, was a revered master. *The Waste Land* was first published in England in 1922 and instantly changed the literary climate. The new young poets found in his work a symbolic vocabulary and a tone of voice much better suited to their needs than Georgian romanticism. It was the difference between 'I must go down to the sea again, to the lonely sea and the sky' and 'Dry bones rattled by the rat's foot year by year'. The dry bones seemed more appropriate: every one of the new young men owed much to Eliot and it was a great shock to the Stalin-worshippers when he finally found haven in, of all things, the Anglican Church.

James Joyce's *Ulysses* was another seminal work. Published in 1922 in Paris, it employed the techniques of the stream of consciousness and the interior monologue to such effect that it seemed to contain a new truth about the human race.

But for me the best prose-writer and the great satirical novelist of the period was Evelyn Waugh. The point about Evelyn Waugh was that he was committed to something so recondite and peculiar, something to do with medieval Christian aristocracy, which had few, if any, representatives in the world around him, that he was free to speak his mind about anything or anybody. It was the inherent third-rateness of our attitudes and institutions which moved him to fury, and laughter was the instrument he chose for his work of demolition. *Decline and Fall* appeared just

Aldous Huxley in 1936. His best-known book *Brave New World* in 1932 took a horrified look at the direction in which he believed society was being led by technological progress. His novels brought an atmosphere of intellectual sophistication to a whole generation. *(Paul Popper Ltd)*

T. S. Eliot, still in his forties, was a revered master in the Thirties. *The Waste Land*, published in England in 1922, had changed the vocabulary and the tone of voice of the next generation of poets. His influence was further reinforced by his work as publisher, editor and critic. *(The Mansell Collection)*

before the decade opened and what it had to say about the English scene was ruthless, hilarious and true. *Vile Bodies* was about the 'bright young things', *Scoop* was about journalism – 'When the exigencies of their employment permitted, Pigge and Corker were friends . . . They had loitered together on many a doorstep and together forced an entry into many a stricken home'. All through the decade he made us grateful to realise how ludicrously horrible the whole set-up was.

P. G. Wodehouse started as a writer of school stories, but came to full bloom in the thirties, with Jeeves and Bertie Wooster, Sir Roderick Glossop, Aunt Agatha and the full benison of the Drones Club. He became a cult.

J. B. Priestley was the great bestseller with *The Good Companions*, a novel about the adventures of a concert-party on the roads of England. It is a good book and has been most unjustly trounced by the sort of critic whose sole criterion of a book's worth is that it should fill the middle class with guilt. *Angel Pavement* was a darker book about claustrophobic life in a small city office. If anybody wants to know what England really seemed to be like at the time as opposed to what it ought to have seemed to be like, he should read Priestley's *English Journey*.

Most people were still reading the older writers. The grand old man was the poet W. B. Yeats, more revered than read by then, though one of his verses from 'The Second Coming' seemed to fit the times, and was always being quoted:

> Things fall apart, the centre cannot hold;
> Mere anarchy is loosed upon the world,
> The blood-dimmed tide is loosed, and everywhere
> The ceremony of innocence is drowned.

Bernard Shaw, the other ancient, was still writing though he had nothing much to say in the Thirties. He enjoyed showing off in the newspapers and he and H. G. Wells, with their commitment to socialism, made a trip to Moscow and came back with tidings of great joy. Bertrand Russell, with his commitment to the truth, went to Moscow too and reported that Stalin was a cruel man and that life in Russia, though Red, was far from rosy. Sound main-line novelists like Arnold Bennett, with their slowly developing dramas of character, were still read but were now definitely old-fashioned. Somerset Maugham's worldly and cynical observations seemed very much of the Twenties and rather French at that.

An uneasiness about the future was slowly percolating through the British mind and people were avid for the facts. Vernon Bartlett's *Germany Explained*, Vera Brittain's *Testament of Youth* and Edgar Mowrer's *Germany Puts the Clock Back* were all bestsellers. Fiction became more factual and ever since Lytton Strachey set the trend with his biography *Queen Victoria* which read like a novel, facts were being presented as if they were fiction. The two great non-musical stage successes of the decade were of this kind. *The Barretts of Wimpole Street* was a dramatised life of Elizabeth Barrett Browning, the poet, and *Richard of Bordeaux* showed Richard II as a young, sensitive, artistic king, frustrated and finally got rid of by a philistine, militaristic nobility. This theme was very much to the taste of the time. Perhaps the best and certainly the most original of the fictionalised biographies was an autobiography of the Roman Emperor Claudius in a series of books *I, Claudius, Claudius the God* by Robert Graves.

The written word was still of great importance in the Thirties and the Left Book Club exerted a strong influence on the mind of the decade, but it was the patriotic musical spectacular *Cavalcade* by Noel Coward, put on at Drury Lane in 1931, which became and remained the testament of the majority.

A very 'Thirties' moment. J. B. Priestley, captain of the Writers XI, tosses for first innings with Gladys Cooper, captain of the Stage team. The occasion is a garden party given in 1932 in aid of the North St Pancras Group Improvement Society. *(Radio Times Hulton Picture Library)*

9 · *Half-time*

In 1935 King George V had been on the throne for twenty-five years. He was a man of simple tastes, fond of the sea and pre-eminent in the annual slaughter of pheasants and partridges. Gruff and sensible, he was very much more to the English taste than any man of ideas or imagination could have been in this position, and in fact he was seen as something of a bulwark against such people. He fitted exactly into the English myth of the 'good old squire' who would look after his own people and his Christmas broadcasts had clinched that impression. He was a genuine father-figure: people felt that they and he had weathered some terrible storms together; it was decided to make a fuss of King George.

If George V was unmistakeably royal, Queen Mary was regal. Tall and impressive and very dignified, she had the royal attribute of appearing to be the one fixed point in a reeling universe. Her skirts had remained at ankle-length through all the vicissitudes of that garment and she wore a splendid kind of hat called a toque which was neither fashionable nor out of fashion, but outside such considerations altogether. The Queen was a woman of considerable taste and her personal raids on the art and antique shops were famous. Both of them were supremely good at their job.

On the day of the Silver Jubilee, Their Majesties drove in procession to St Paul's for a thanksgiving service and received loyal addresses from the Houses of Parliament. London was floodlit, something quite new; there were flags and banners everywhere and, as the King wrote, 'the greatest number of people in the streets that I have ever seen in my life'. When they toured the London slums they received, to the King's great surprise, an overwhelmingly affectionate and enthusiastic welcome. 'I am beginning to think they must like me for myself' he is supposed to have said.

The celebrations were sincere and heartfelt and most of Their Majesties' subjects would have been very willing to return to the earlier, simpler Britain of which the Royal Family reminded them.

Stanley Baldwin succeeded Ramsay MacDonald: masterly inactivity gave way to total inertia. And now the situation in Europe took a turn for the worse. Up to the Silver Jubilee in 1935 it had been possible for an optimist to believe that another war might be avoided, but now the latent terror and violence in Europe began to take dramatic shape on the world stage.

Mussolini had been Dictator (Il Duce, the Leader) in Italy since 1922 when his march on Rome, made smooth by liberal doses of castor-oil poured down the throats of his opponents, had got him to the top. Il Duce (regularly pronounced in England like an unexpected echo of Wellington, the Deuce) was a sanguine man, originally a Socialist, but now possessed of a Roman dream: the Italians were all to retrace their steps until they became once again the virile legionaries their ancestors had been, with Mussolini in the role of Caesar. As Caesar, he required an Empire and in October 1935 he marched into Abyssinia to take one.

This action was meant to give notice of the rebirth of Italy as a martial nation since the last time they had marched into Abyssinia looking for glory, the Abyssinians had thrashed them at the Battle of Adowa in 1896, and of the Italians who escaped death on that occasion, few returned with their virility intact owing to the peculiar trophy-hunting habits of the mountain tribes. This time, Mussolini reckoned, the new toys of the twentieth century – the tanks, the war-planes, the bombs and the gas – would redress the balance and he proved to be right.

It was a shameful war. The Abyssinians were ill-equipped even as guerillas and on the high plateau a kind of monsoon wind blows steadily at a time when the long African grass is ripe and dry. A line of incendiary bombs dropped across the direction of the wind could set a whole province ablaze and consume everything, men, women, children and animals. Rebellious chiefs were dealt with by being dropped from aeroplanes into the middle of squares formed of their supporters in their own villages. Gas was used. Bruno Mussolini, the Duce's son, gave ecstatic descriptions of the effects of bombs dropped on groups of people: 'When the bomb drops, the group explodes like a flower' he said. They had a general called 'Electric Whiskers' and these lovable exploits of his were given world-wide publicity by the Italians who wished it to

Overleaf

In 1935 George V had been on the throne for 25 years and the nation decided to give him a party. The Jubilee celebrations were marked by genuine warmth of feeling, which came as a surprise to the King himself. Here vast crowds cheer the procession as it returns to the Palace. *(Keystone Press Agency Ltd)*

TOURS &
CANADIAN PACIFIC
SUN
INSURANCE OFFICE
THE OLDEST INSURANCE
OFFICE IN THE WORLD
225 YEARS OF SERVICE
"BLACK
& WHITE"

be known that they had caught up with the Joneses: at last they were in the twentieth century.

One of the first towns to fall was Adowa, and the French and British Governments conceived the idea that, since the old humiliation had now been avenged, they might be able to come to an agreement between the Abyssinians and the Italians. Accordingly Sir Samuel Hoare, the Foreign Secretary, and Pierre Laval for France concocted a plan which ceded most of Abyssinia to the Italians. Unfortunately for them, the plan was leaked to the Press

A Jubilee street party in Battersea. Every back street was decked out with red, white and blue bunting, and schoolchildren were given special Jubilee mugs. Union Jacks and firework displays were the order of the day throughout the country. *(Radio Times Hulton Picture Library)*

before any government had approved it and there was a great outcry. Sir Samuel was made the scapegoat and wept in the House of Commons. Then he went abroad for a holiday and returned to another Ministry. Anthony Eden succeeded him at the Foreign Office and helped to persuade the League of Nations to impose economic sanctions. These made no difference at all to the supply of oil and petrol for the Italian tanks and aeroplanes, and the idea that the heroic Ethiopian guerillas under their mediaeval Rases (barons) and with their job-lot of European instructors 'would give Mussolini something to think about' proved ill-founded. The Abyssinian Army was caught up in a pitched battle early in 1936 and soundly defeated. The Emperor Haile Selassie, King of Kings, Lion of Judah, left the country and came to live in England, setting up house at Bath.

There was much sympathy for Haile Selassie: he was romantic in the English fashion, with a 'Pageant of History' all of his own since he claimed descent from Solomon and the Queen of Sheba. But the political organisation of his country had remained much

The Dictators and their henchmen were joyously seized on by David Low, the great New Zealand-born cartoonist of the *Evening Standard.* Here Hitler, Goering and Goebbels wave goodbye as Mussolini sets out for Abyssinia, leaving the field free for the Nazis in Europe. *(London Express Pictures)*

the same as England's had been in King John's time, with the Rases owing allegiance to the King but as often as not failing to turn up with their armies to support him in a crisis, preferring to sit on the fence until they saw which way the victory was likely to go. Many of them accepted bribes and never marched. Some fought for the Italians. The obvious lesson to be learned from this war was that the League of Nations had not been capable of preventing Italian aggressors from over-running Abyssinia, and Hitler was not slow to learn it.

Stanley Baldwin and Sir Samuel Hoare, his Foreign Secretary, in 1935. The outcry after the discovery of the Hoare-Laval Pact, a secret treaty which proposed to cede most of Abyssinia to Mussolini, wiped the bright smile from Sir Samuel's countenance. *(Keystone Press Agency Ltd)*

The German Rhineland had been designated by the Versailles Treaty a demilitarised zone. Now, in 1936, Hitler sent his troops in to re-occupy it. He was so sure that nothing would be done to prevent him that no ammunition was issued to his army of occupation. He was right. Britain did nothing, France did nothing. It was obvious now that no-one would stand up for anything. Appeasement had begun.

10 · Royal Occasions

At five minutes to midnight on 20 January 1936, King George died at Sandringham in Norfolk, the scene of many of his sporting triumphs, and Queen Mary turned from the bedside to kiss the hand of the new sovereign, her son David, who had been Prince of Wales and was now to be known as Edward VIII. The public had been well prepared for the death of the King and a few hours earlier the golden voice of Stuart Hibberd, the BBC's chief announcer, had told the country 'The King's life is moving peacefully towards its close'.

King George was sincerely mourned as the representative of tradition, stability and 'the good old days'. This was the end of an era and the fact had been brought home by the death of Rudyard Kipling two days earlier. Vast crowds waited all night on the pavements to watch the old King's funeral. As the coffin with the crown on top was drawn through the streets of London on a gun-carriage with the new King and five other monarchs walking behind it, something strange happened: the top fell off the crown and rolled in the roadway. It was a Maltese cross formed of a huge sapphire with diamonds and it lay in the gutter for several seconds, until a sergeant-major picked it up and put it in his pocket. This was afterwards widely regarded as an omen or portent of the tragedy which was to follow.

The new King had a very different image from his father's. His role in life had been Prince Charming and in this part he had been highly successful in 'cementing the ties of Empire'. He had been seen dancing in night-clubs and road-houses, went around with girls a good deal and had broken his collarbone while foxhunting. It was not only in the Empire that he had done something to redeem the archaic image of the Royal Family; he was the pet of the younger generation in Britain and something of a hero among the unemployed. Once, when he was touring the South Wales coalfields, appalled by the squalid misery around him, he had told an unemployed miner 'something must be done' to the great um-

The TATLER

Vol. CXXXIX. No. 1806. London, February 5, 1936 POSTAGE: Inland, 1½d.; Canada and Newfoundland, 1½d.; Foreign, 3d. Price One Shilling

H.M. THE KING WITH THE DUKES OF YORK AND GLOUCESTER

In setting this picture in the forefront of the number that shows the funeral of our late beloved King, we wish to say no more than to express our humble and loyal sympathy with His Majesty and the sorrowing Royal family over an irreparable loss the whole Empire shares. It is furthermore a sympathy which has been given world-wide expression

The frontispiece of *The Tatler* of 5 February, 1936, shows Edward VIII walking in his father's funeral procession, flanked by his brothers the Duke of York (later King George VI) and the Duke of Gloucester. The crowd stood all night in freezing January weather to wait for the cortege to go by. By the time the coffin passed they numbered two million. *(John Frost—Historical Newspaper Services)* brage of the politicians, who wanted none of that sort of talk. To that one sentence he owed most of his reputation among them as 'irresponsible'. Though forty years old at his accession, he had retained a remarkably youthful, even adolescent, appearance, with a sort of wistful diffidence and a distaste for Royal occasions and attitudes which was to do him no good among the veteran officials of the Court. One of his early acts as King was to compress a morning of loyal addresses into a few minutes by receiving all the delegates at once, en bloc. He had other strange and disconcerting habits: little dinners in London flats with his friends, walking to appointments in London through the rain, digging in the garden stripped to the waist at his retreat, Fort Belvedere, in Windsor Great Park. Heads were shaken, and that they were grey heads was all the more dangerous. Orwell was not altogether wrong when he said that in the Thirties England was a land of snobbery and privilege, ruled largely by the old and silly. Their hackles were now rising.

Within a few months of his accession, it was known in some society and political circles that he proposed to marry Mrs Wallis Simpson, an American from Baltimore, who had divorced one

By the end of 1936 the Abdication crisis was on. There was much sympathy for the King and sporadic demonstrations in his support, but they were largely spontaneous and unorganised and gave the authorities little trouble. *(Radio Times Hulton Picture Library)*

husband and was now in process of divorcing another, Ernest Simpson, an English shipbroker, who had spent most of his life in the United States. The remarkable affair of Wallis Simpson and the Prince of Wales could be laid at the door of Lady Furness, one of the celebrated Morgan sisters, who was a very good friend of the Prince. When she had to go back to the United States on business she told her friend, Mrs Simpson: 'You look after him while I'm away. See that he doesn't get into any mischief.' All she could say when she returned and saw what had happened was 'Wallis, of all people!'. And that seemed to fit the case. On the surface, the whole affair was inexplicable. Wallis Warfield, as she originally was, seemed to be a goodlooking American woman (but nothing spectacular) chiefly remarkable for being neat and composed, with no hair out of place and a rather governessy expression.

Millions of words have been written in explanation of this worldshaking affair, and American friends of mine cling to this day to the theory that only some shared sexual deviation could explain Edward's insistence on a world well lost for love. In the Thirties we thought Freud could explain everything. I don't

The new Royal Family presented an image of contented domesticity. Here they are with four dogs, two of them corgis, outside the children's playhouse at Royal Lodge, Windsor. Their life style was very much more to the British taste than the flavour of international high living which had attached to Edward VIII. *(Radio Times Hulton Picture Library)*

believe it. I think the King, who had played Prince Charming to a full house with rapturous applause all over the world, had only been able to do it because he was a very ordinary young man. He had had to be a good mixer, and at the same time completely apart. He had been deprived of his birthright of ordinariness and Wallis, ordinary herself, gave it back to him. It was, in fact, a simple case of delayed adolescent romantic love, and I think Ernest Simpson, who to my mind is the graceful hero of the whole affair, knew this well enough: he used to refer to the Prince of Wales as 'Peter Pan'. Years later Wallis wrote of Edward: 'Over and above the charm of his personality and the warmth of his manner, he was the open sesame to a new and glittering world that excited me as nothing in my life had done before . . . All I can say is that it was like being Wallis in Wonderland.'

By the time of Edward's accession, the whole situation was irreparable. The British Press printed nothing on the subject and continued to enact the gentleman's agreement until the eleventh hour, but on the Continent and in the United States it was the biggest newspaper scandal of the century, and British citizens living abroad were bombarding the House of Commons with complaints and demands for an explanation. King Edward and Mrs Simpson went for a cruise in the Mediterranean while the Simpsons' divorce case began at Ipswich, where it was hoped it would not be noticed. When they returned, Stanley Baldwin turned up one morning to see the King secretly at Fort Belvedere and tried to persuade him that Mrs Simpson should drop her divorce petition. The King replied that he had no right to interfere with the affairs of an individual. Mrs Simpson received her decree nisi in October.

In November the King, alerted to the true situation in the Commons and the Commonwealth by a letter from his Private Secretary which implored him to send Mrs Simpson abroad, sent for Baldwin and told him 'I am going to marry Mrs Simpson and I am prepared to go'. He proposed a morganatic marriage, which suggestion he was prepared to submit to the Cabinet and all the Commonwealth Cabinets. He thus delivered himself into the hands of Mr Baldwin, who informed him that the lady that he married must automatically become the Queen. How much longer the Press would have possessed itself in superhuman patience cannot be guessed. In fact they were let off the hook by a saintly innocent, Dr Blunt the Bishop of Bradford, who had never heard of Mrs Simpson. At a Diocesan Conference the Bishop said he wished the King 'would show more positive evidence of his awareness of the need for Divine Guidance'. All he meant was that the King ought to go to church, but it was enough. The Press interpreted his words as an official breaking of the silence and leapt, unleashed, upon its prey. Mrs Simpson fled to Cannes: the King, besieged at Fort Belvedere, clung to his morganatic dream until Mr Baldwin demolished it in a public statement: 'There is no such thing as what is called morganatic marriage known to our law ... The lady whom he marries, by the fact of her marriage to the King, necessarily becomes Queen ... The only way in which this result could be avoided would be by legislation dealing with a particular case. His Majesty's Government are not prepared to introduce such legislation.'

There was some support for the King, some of it welcome from Churchill and Duff Cooper and the Beaverbrook and the Rothermere Press, some extremely unwelcome – Mosley's Blackshirts marched up and down Whitehall with a picture of the King chanting 'One, two, three, four, five, we want Baldwin dead or alive'. But it was too late, it was uncoordinated and it was useless.

The King signed the Instrument of Abdication, condemning his nervous, shy, retiring brother, the Duke of York, to coronation as George VI – the wretched man burst into tears when he heard his fate – and then delivered a farewell broadcast to the nation in the voice of an angry man at the end of his tether, declaring that he could not discharge his duties as King 'without the help and support of the woman I love'. He left England as Duke of Windsor in the destroyer *Fury*, to stay with Baron Eugene de Rothschild in Austria.

So George VI was eventually crowned and lived with his charming wife and their two little Princesses, Elizabeth and Margaret, to be, as it has been said, 'the first happy family to have its home in Buckingham Palace since it was built'.

11 · *The Rehearsal*

During 1936, the year when three Kings reigned in Britain, though the Depression was well past its peak and the figures for unemployment were improving, the political sky outside grew darker. It was obvious to the Foreign Office that Hitler and Mussolini were drawing closer together and it rightly believed that Hitler had his eye on Austria. It was also obvious that almost nothing could be done about this situation, but it did that almost nothing by sending Lord Halifax, a puritanical High Churchman, a man who has been described as 'a long drink of cold water', on a hunting expedition with, of all people, Hermann Goering, the fat and ruthless adventurer who was to be Hitler's Marshal in charge of the Nazi Air Force. What these two can have had to say to each other is beyond human imagination, and nothing came of it but some comic pictures published in the Press of Lord Halifax, drooping with gloom, all six and a half feet of him, and wearing above his disapproving features a series of laughable hats, of the kind decreed for hunting by German enthusiasts. As a spectacle, these were soon eclipsed by the opening of the Surrealist Art Exhibition in July when Salvador Dali, the high priest of the movement, appeared in a diving suit with a motorcar radiator cap on top, and had to be rescued from suffocation while trying to make a speech inside it.

The subconscious, Freud's discovery from Vienna, was the true begetter of the Surrealist Movement, which was at least ten years out of date in Paris, but new to the London scene. The Surrealists say that the world of the unconscious is more real than the world on the surface, and that the juxtaposition of images occurring in that part of the mind expresses what the artist truly means to say better than any design he can arrive at by simple intuition and thought. Moreover, something not himself, something like the 'collective unconscious', can take a hand in painting the picture. All art owes something to the subconscious mind, but Surrealism is a sort of distillation which owes everything. Lewis Carroll in the

Alice books and Edward Lear in his nonsense poems are claimed by the Surrealists to be of their movement.

Significantly, because the decade was now on the brink of a climax, the Exhibition was a pageant of dread or 'angst', as it was fashionable to call it: the Thirties' subconscious certainly had nothing cheerful to say. Sex seemed to be the seat of most anxieties but some of the paintings, like the Magrittes, depicted much newer preoccupations. Dali's soft watches draped over angular surfaces gave everyone a jolt of insecurity ending in a laugh, but one of his pictures of two crippled monsters destroying each other was a remarkable feat of his agile subconscious. It was prophetic.

The Spanish Civil War broke out in July. It was at once acknowledged as the showdown between the Left and the Right in Europe, and acclaimed by both sides as the great Crusade of their time. It was really a war about the fate of Spain, fought out by

Salvador Dali in a deep diving suit crowned with a cocktail glass was the *pièce de resistance* at the opening of the Surrealist Exhibition in London in July 1936. He had to be rescued from suffocation in his chosen costume. *(Madame Nane Poirson)*

Spaniards to the bitter end. Spain had legally elected a government of the Left, and one Major Franco raised the standard of rebellion against it, for the Catholic Church against godless Communism, with Moslem troops from Spanish Morocco. Not least among the defenders of democratic law and order were the Anarchists of Catalonia. In spite of the legitimacy of the Spanish Government, the British Government fell into the pious posture of non-intervention once more and persuaded twenty-seven other Governments to back this principle officially, though many of them in fact did intervene. An amateur 'International Brigade' arrived quite early in the conflict: it is estimated that 2,762 British volunteers fought in Spain and 543 died there.

In most civil wars, the propagandists of both sides are never short of atrocities to stir up hatred, but the war in Spain broke all records for savagery. Most of the British popular Press was on the whole for the Republicans, but for Conservative organs they were always 'the Reds' or 'the Communists' though in fact they ranged through the whole spectrum, from anarchists to mild social democrats. To many people of my generation the Spanish Civil War was and remained the most significant and deeply felt experience of their lives. This was particularly true of the mostly middle-class associates and sympathisers with the young poets and intellectuals of the Thirties movement, many of whom were profoundly changed by their experience.

In England communication across the class gap in the Thirties was almost impossible. In Spain, in this respect, everything was suddenly simple. Most of the men who fought had brought themselves to see the war as a straight confrontation between good and evil. It was quite easy to dodge the non-intervention authorities: the arrangements were mostly in the hands of the Communist Parties of Britain and France and once you presented yourself at one of their recruiting offices, you could be on your way into battle within a few hours. At the frontier your guilty, resentful, socially selfconscious little personality fell away, and you were reborn across the border as a man and a brother. It was like an absolution and if the worker with whom you fought shoulder to shoulder happened to be Spanish the rebirth was total, because the tangle of conscience-stricken class feelings the British carried about with them was incomprehensible to him.

Government troops surrender to Nationalist forces on a front in Northern Spain. For foreigners who fought in the Spanish War, the main impact was not so much the experience of battle as the bitterness of this family quarrel and the enormous numbers of people executed on both sides. *(Keystone Press Agency Ltd)*

But that first ecstatic sense of catharsis did not long survive in most of the intellectual volunteers. The fact is that Spain turned out to be altogether too foreign: the feelings which drove the Spaniards to massacre each other in droves turned out to have little or no bearing on those which had inspired the idealism of the British Left, most of which was derived from the protestant Christian conscience. To take as examples only the chief priests of the movement, Auden, Spender, Day Lewis and MacNeice: all of them emerged from devout homes, and two of them from clerical backgrounds. Claude Cockburn, an active Communist in the Thirties, has put it on record that he first became aware of feelings which were to lead him to Communism when singing the Magnificat in the school chapel. That the public school ethics of fair play and esprit de corps had played a large part in the formation of the minds which launched the Thirties movement is obvious from their works, and the British Labour movement has always owed more to Methodism than to Marx. This conscience-picking idealism was utterly alien to the Spaniards fighting their private war. Eighty-five per cent of them more or less illiterate peasants and fifteen per cent upper crust, their motives were personal, local, regional and sectarian. Communists had no hesitation in shooting Anarchists to gain control of a local situation.

The foreign comrades were slow to realise that, say, the Asturias and Catalonia were not divisions like English counties, but furiously jealous little nations. Enormous numbers of Spaniards, hundreds of thousands, died by execution on both sides. They were 'tried' in batches by 'courts' consisting of a 'comrades committee' or a 'court martial' convened on the spot and shot within a few minutes. This procedure applied even to men ostensibly on the same side – 'Trotskyite traitor' was a common verdict. It was the sight and sound of these daily mass-executions which revolted the civilised Western participants. Was this the Revolution which they had willed? Was there any real connection between this vindictive bloody mess and the social justice to which they were committed? Many of them had second thoughts.

Most of the British soldiers of the International Brigade, of course, were workers, many of them unemployed miners, and their convictions had been built in over generations of deprivation. Franco had had a promise of support from Mussolini before the war began and ideological allies had supplied him with arms from the beginning, in spite of the elaborate precautions of the League's Non-Intervention Committee. But when Italian troops moved in on Franco's side, the Left redoubled its efforts to rally support for the Republicans. Writers and painters all over Europe set to work as propagandists. By the spring of 1937 there were 30,000 Germans and 80,000 Italians in Spain. The Germans marched and, worse, flew aeroplanes. The Republicans had practically no aircraft and huge sums of money were paid to freelance pilots by the Spanish Government. The deliberate bombing of civilians was regarded in those quaint old days as an unimaginable barbarity. When the Germans bombed the Basque town of Guernica for Franco and practically wiped it out, the whole world was outraged and Picasso's picture went on tour all over Europe, including England. Now everybody seemed to be taking a hand in the war. The International Brigades had volunteers from dozens of countries, including two British contingents, one of them oddly named after the mild Mr Attlee.

The Spanish Civil War was to continue until 1939, but most of the surviving British volunteers of the International Brigade came back home in 1937. They had had a rough war. Twenty per cent of the entire British force had been killed and more than seventy-five per cent were wounded. Even as they disembarked from the ferry giving their clenched-fist salute for the Press photographers, it was clear that the result of the Great Confrontation between Good and Evil was a victory for Evil, and now new doubts set in. Had it been, in fact, the Great Confrontation? It was beginning to look more like the dress rehearsal for something much worse.

The Fascists, at any rate, had been greatly encouraged by their adventure in Spain. Hitler and Mussolini, now 'the Rome-Berlin Axis', began a gigantic build-up of their armed forces. Hitler rightly interpreted the farce which non-intervention had turned out to be as the green light, but he evidently needed more time to prepare for his career of conquest and when, in 1937, his aeroplanes wiped out the Basque cultural capital, Guernica, and most of its inhabitants and the whole world turned to revile him, his propaganda machine under Dr Goebbels – instead of brazening it out – went into a fury of action to try to convince everybody that the Basques had blown up their own city in order to discredit General Franco.

12 · *Comings and Goings*

Late in 1937, in the brief interval before the curtain rose on the last act, this was the state of play. Two wars were in progress, the Spanish Civil War which it now seemed clear Franco was going to win, and a new one in the Far East between Japan and China. Japan had marched in and taken Pekin. Britain, although she had important commercial interests in China, was not strong enough in the Far East to take on Japan.

It never occurred for a moment to anybody that the French behind their Maginot Line, an impregnably fortified strip stretching all across northern France to the Belgian border with hundreds of miles of underground workings, might turn out not to be a tower of military strength and virtue and the West's main guarantor on land.

Britain had been rearming, though by no means feverishly, since 1935, but there were still 1,600,000 unemployed. On the other side of that penny, 2,400,000 motor licences were issued in 1938. We had a new man at the War Office. Leslie Hore-Belisha, a most intelligent and modern-minded Minister, was trying hard to bring the Army up to date. He made Army life considerably less uncomfortably barbaric, and had a plan for giving commissions to intelligent NCOs. The fury of the generals against him knew no bounds and it didn't help that he was Jewish. He was defeated in the end by the 'well-bred horse' syndrome and elbowed out.

There had been a large influx of refugees from Europe, mostly Jewish, into this country, so large as to be noticeable among the crowds in the London streets. It has been said of the Nazis that they were always most at war with the human mind and the number of intellectuals among the refugees was disproportionately large; our universities were the gainers, particularly in the sciences, though the newcomers had very little to do with the most shattering of all the scientific discoveries of the century: the atom had already been split at Cambridge and it was known to a handful of our best physicists that it might be possible to make an atomic bomb.

The ordinary refugees were unpopular, but not violently so, The London attitude seemed to be much the same as Duff Cooper's who once announced 'Although I loathe anti-semitism, I do dislike Jews'. A well-known bus conductor on the Swiss Cottage run expressed his feelings by providing a free translation and always bawled out 'Swiss Cottage – Kleine Schweizer-Haus'.

Above all, we had a new Prime Minister. After the Coronation, Stanley Baldwin had relinquished office to Neville Chamberlain and, as Lord Baldwin of Bewdley, disappeared into his beloved countryside to become a rustic worthy. Many rude criticisms have been levelled at Mr Baldwin and certainly his chief influence had been anaesthetic. Stability and the status quo had been obsessions he shared with the great majority of voters throughout the Thirties and, unless circumstances forced him into action, he had preferred to drowse. He had a genuine poetic passion for the idea of England and it must have gone against the grain with him to do absolutely nothing for the unemployed, but that is what he did. It may be that to his deep-rooted aversion to confrontation, his

A mortar section in action in army manoeuvres in Hertfordshire in the summer of 1937. The farm workers belong to the old, slow, country England which had changed very little since Victorian times. The scythe was still more common than the combine harvester. *(Radio Times Hulton Picture Library)*

genius for keeping antagonisms safely in solution and never allowing them to crystallise out, we may owe the fact that, when finally we had to go to war, we went as one people, an undivided nation.

Apart from being another Conservative Midlands industrialist, the new Prime Minister had little in common with the old one. Neville Chamberlain was an upright provincial businessman with an old-fashioned moustache who had once been Lord Mayor of Birmingham, and whose qualities of vision and imagination seemed admirably to suit him for such a position. A political observer at the time he became Prime Minister wrote of him: 'This seeming lack of breadth of mind and culture . . . arouses some misgivings about Mr Chamberlain. Clarity of mind – and he has it in an unusual degree – is not enough if the mind, so to say, sees the field with searching clearness, but not the field as part of the landscape, and that kind of limited vision is not necessarily compensated by courage such as Mr Chamberlain has. The two together could be a positive danger.'

Mr Baldwin had not been fond of first-class minds: Mr Chamberlain's Cabinet excluded most of the able men so that by

From the mid-Thirties onwards the trickle of refugees from Europe became a steady stream. These Jewish boys from Germany and Austria have come up from their base camp at Dovercourt to spend the Christmas of 1938 in London with foster-parents. The Continental cut of the refugees' clothes made them conspicuous among the London crowds. *(Keystone Press Agency Ltd)*

1938 Churchill, Eden, Duff Cooper, Macmillan and Amery formed a small Conservative opposition inside the Conservative party. The old gang, Lord Halifax, Sir John Simon and Sir Samuel Hoare, were given the jobs. One Minister, Sir Thomas Inskip, was a man of such natural endowments that when his appointment as Minister of Defence was announced, the House of Commons sat there laughing for several minutes. In that company, Anthony Eden – still, but not for long at the Foreign Office – resembled at forty some species of whizz-kid.

Baldwin had preferred to leave his Ministers to their own devices – to a criminal extent, it was sometimes said – but Chamberlain was an interfering Prime Minister: he liked, he said, to give each of his Ministers a policy and it was in foreign affairs that he chiefly meddled because, though he had little experience in that field, he had a foreign policy and it was not the same as Eden's.

That policy was the line that came to be known as 'appeasement'. There was nothing new in it: it was believed by almost every liberal mind in Britain that the Versailles Treaty had been unjustly harsh to the Germans and that some kind of 'give and take' policy might have modified the explosive situation in Europe. Eden was contemptuous of Italy and was pursuing a strong line on non-intervention, insisting that the Germans and the Italians should take their promises not to interfere in the Spanish Civil War seriously. Chamberlain thought Eden was being inconsiderate to Italy and set about conciliating Mussolini, and this involved accepting the Duce's conquest of Abyssinia. Finally, in a conversation between Grandi, the Italian Ambassador, and Eden and Chamberlain together, Chamberlain actually argued Grandi's case for him against Eden. Eden resigned in February 1938 and Lord Halifax, who had no objection to letting Chamberlain run the Foreign Office, was made Foreign Secretary.

Hitler had never made a secret of the fact that his dearest ambition was to bring about a merger or 'Anschluss' between Germany and Austria and on 11 March 1938 he marched across the frontier and swallowed up Austria into the German Reich. Vast crowds, hysterical with joy, lined the streets to welcome his advance and the redeeming of the promise 'Ein Volk, Ein Reich, Ein Führer'.

Chamberlain seemed affronted less by the deed than by its manner of accomplishment. Unaccompanied by conferences, acts of diplomacy or committee-work, a simple snatch, it was outside any frame of reference known to him. He made disapproving noises but did nothing. It has been fashionable ever since to sneer at

Chamberlain's appeasement, but in 1938 he must have felt that he had very good reasons to play for time: it had been estimated by the best available experts that on the outbreak of war the German Air Force would be able to deliver 600 tons of high explosive bombs over Britain every day, and that each ton would kill sixteen people, so that in the first month of hostilities about 300,000 British people would die in air raids. In fact this estimate turned out to be wildly wrong. Even later, when they had bases in France, the Germans were never able to approach this weight of bombardment and, in the event, in the Second World War the death rate turned out to be not sixteen persons but one person per ton of high explosive delivered. Gas had been the most dreaded of the weapons of the First World War and everybody I knew expected to be choking to death in the street within an hour of a declaration of war.

So Chamberlain did nothing and though Churchill thundered he was out of office, isolated and generally regarded, even by his own party, as a dangerous reactionary. Up and down the country nobody cared very much about the Anschluss. Austria was barely viable as a country anyhow – it was the rump of the old Austro-Hungarian Empire which had disintegrated in the First World War. The Austrian, after all, was a sort of German – but with qualities of humour, elegance and light-mindedness: Strauss-like qualities. Well, if they wanted to be German, no accounting for tastes, good luck to them: at least they might leaven the lump.

But now Hitler was presented with another group of 'Volk' who could be persuaded to clamour for the Reich and the Führer. Czechoslovakia had been created in 1919 and had been given a great curved fringe of mountain territory at its Western end to form a defensible frontier. This fringe, the Sudetenland, largely inhabited by Germans in defiance of the principles of self-determination, jutted out into Austria and contained a very strong line of fortified defensive positions. Financed by Berlin, the Sudeten Germans now began to scream for justice.

By August their screaming had reached such a pitch that Chamberlain was convinced it was a threat to peace and sent Walter Runciman, the villain of the Jarrow March, to investigate the situation on the spot. The Czechs did not want Runciman, whose very presence seemed to suggest doubts about their title to the Sudetenland, but Chamberlain told them that Britain could not be expected to care very much about what happened to them unless the investigation went through. Runciman stayed until September, by which time the demands of the Sudeten Germans, prompted by Hitler, had been stepped up to such an extent that it seemed that only 'a transfer of territory', as *The Times* put it, would satisfy them. Chamberlain did not accept this, but on 15 September he flew to Berchtesgaden to meet Hitler and finally conceded the principle that Czech territory should be transferred to Germany.

So began the most macabre of all the Thirties spectaculars: the spectacle of Mr Chamberlain, with his umbrella and his winged collar and his thin smile, flying about through the skies of Europe like some great black stork of ill-omen, smoothing Hitler's path, and all with the best of motives.

The young general Keitel, one of the Führer's entourage whom Chamberlain met at Berchtesgaden, must have been doing his homework until very late at night when he thought of the number of divisions he would need to crack the Czech defence system which was, by all accounts, almost of Maginot Line quality. In the event, Mr Chamberlain was there to tell his Fuhrer that he could have what he wanted without the trouble of fighting for it.

Chamberlain returned from Berchtesgaden to a round of diplomatic activity with the object of persuading the French, who had a treaty with Czechoslovakia, to forget it. They did not need

Hitler leads Neville Chamberlain past the guard of honour as he arrives in Munich in October 1938. Ribbentrop is on the right, and Sir Neville Henderson walks a pace behind. The swastika flag and the Union Jack wave together for the last time. *(Radio Times Hulton Picture Library)*

much persuading because the cession of the Sudetenland to Germany would not affect their strategy, which was simply to sit behind their Maginot Line until the crack of doom. Hitler, meanwhile, had been drawing up on a map a sort of menu of the meal he now expected the Czechs to serve up to him. When this document was ready, Chamberlain flew to meet Hitler again at Godesberg and examine it. He found it objectionable: not only were the inhabitants of ceded areas to have no choice of staying or leaving, but certain territories Hitler had marked for his own had Czech, not German, majorities.

Chamberlain flew home again and now it seemed that at last he was going to stand firm, promise support to the Czechs and persuade the French to honour their treaty obligations. The British Fleet was mobilised on 28 September and when Parliament was assembled Chamberlain made a speech whose whole drift seemed to be pointing towards war. But before he reached the climax there was a dramatic interruption. A messenger handed him a note which, after glancing at, he read out to the House. It was Hitler's invitation to a further meeting at Munich.

What exactly Chamberlain thought he could accomplish by his missions of appeasement is not clear to this day, except on the assumption that he suffered from the great delusion that Hitler was an ordinary, reasonable man and as such would prefer not to go to war if he could avoid it. This delusion, which was just possible for a provincial British Islander, was incredible on the Continent where they were used to the Germans, to the Nazi mentality and to Real Politik, and had taken Hitler's measure years before. When Chamberlain said 'How terrible, fantastic, incredible it is that we should be digging trenches and trying out gas masks here because of a quarrel in a far away country between people of whom we know nothing', he was certainly speaking for the ordinary people of Britain but, coming from a man who at this dreadful juncture in history could throw the whole giant weight of the British Empire into the scales, the lines seemed to have a naive, bleating quality.

It was, in fact, a tone of voice which chimed exactly with the contemporary mood. Britain was suffering in the summer of 1938 from a mild panic. The Anschluss hadn't bothered them much, but the evidence that the authorities were taking it so seriously did bother them. The aid-raid precautions, the sandbagged buildings, the parks made hideous with slit trenches, soldiers suddenly in authority, new officials of organisations known only by their absurd initials and apparently in a position to order people about:

all this was seen as sinister. The Press and even some of the experts had printed gross exaggerations of the effects of air-raids. It was widely believed that half a million people would perish on the first day of the war. The precautions reassured nobody; they confirmed our worst fears.

When Chamberlain flew to Munich, he was given a tremendous send-off. Sixteen Ministers had agreed among themselves to be at the airport to wish him well. The High Commissioners of Canada, Australia and Eire were there, and many members of the Diplomatic Corps including the French Ambassador, the Italian Ambassador and the German Chargé d'Affaires. As he climbed into the aeroplane a great cheer went up.

On the Continent the wits were already at work: one story was that Haile Selassie of Abyssinia had written to the Czech President, Benes: 'I hear you are receiving the support of the British Government. You have my profound sympathy.'

At Munich on 30 September the French and British did not resist the German claims, except to ask for plebiscites in doubtful areas. They even agreed that the Germans should take over a large slice of territory almost immediately, so that the Czechs lost not only their defensive system but most of its equipment as well. The Czechs did not take part in the conference. They were told of the result afterwards. One of them said to a French delegate: 'When your time comes, you will ask "Where are those two million Czechs who might have been fighting with us?"'

Hitler and Chamberlain signed a separate document declaring that their countries would never go to war with each other. Waved by Chamberlain on his return to London, this document procured for him so ecstatic a reception that one disenchanted observer said 'I thought they were going to grovel on the ground in front of him'. Chamberlain's own account of his return reads: 'Even the descriptions in the papers give no idea of the scenes in the streets as I drove from Heston to the Palace. They were lined from one end to the other with people of every class, shouting themselves hoarse, leaping on the running board, banging on the windows and thrusting their hands into the car to be shaken. The scenes culminated in Downing Street, when I spoke to the multitude below from the same window, I believe, as that from which Dizzy announced peace with honour sixty years ago.' Chamberlain, nevertheless, did not abate the rearmament programme.

The euphoria of relief. On his return to Heston Airport from Munich with a piece of paper signed by Hitler, Chamberlain received a tremendous ovation and huge crowds followed him to Downing Street, where he addressed them from a balcony. The large smiling face behind belongs to Leslie Hore-Belisha, Minister of War. *(Keystone Press Agency Ltd)*

13 · Waiting for the End, Boys

Only a very few days after Chamberlain returned from Munich, a public opinion poll revealed that very few people believed that Hitler would keep his promise. It was not any more a question of if but when war would break out. A dreamlike state prevailed in Great Britain, a sort of mesmerised fatalism possessed the average citizen's mind. People did what they had always done, but absent-mindedly, with the inner ear cocked for the messages which would send their spirits, like rabbits, scuttling for cover. But the first of these was not to arrive until the New Year.

On 10 March Sir Samuel Hoare chose a rather unpropitious moment to announce his own recovery from shock, making a speech in which he hoped that a new era of peace and prosperity was about to begin. Five days later Hitler marched into Prague and swallowed up the defenceless remains of Czechoslovakia. Only Chamberlain was surprised. 'Is this an attempt to dominate the world by force?' he asked. Britain and France had promised the Czech representatives that they would defend the remnants of Czechoslovakia. Now they said that no such guarantees could apply to a state which no longer existed. Chamberlain denounced Hitler's action and gave guarantees to Poland, Rumania and Greece. Lithuania surrendered the former German city of Memel to Hitler on 22 March, after an ultimatum. On 5 April the Italians began the bombing of Albanian towns without warning and King Zog of Albania fled to the West.

By now Britain was prepared to fight, but the situation was sadly different from what it had been in 1938. Churchill was one of the few to appreciate to the full that difference.

The subjugation of Czechoslovakia robbed the Allies of the Czech

Overleaf
In February 1939 a general distribution of air-raid shelters began. Here the inhabitants of a little street in North London turn out to welcome their steel Anderson shelters, which were dug into the tiny back gardens. *(Radio Times Hulton Picture Library)*

Army of twenty-one regular divisions, fifteen or sixteen second-line divisions already mobilised, and also their mountain fortress line, which in the days of Munich had required the deployment of thirty German divisions or the main strength of the mobile and fully trained German Army. According to Generals Halder and Jodl, there were but thirteen German divisions, of which only five were composed of first-line troops, left in the West at the time of the Munich arrangement. We certainly suffered a loss through the fall of Czechoslovakia equivalent to some thirty-five divisions. Besides this the Skoda works, the second most important arsenal in central Europe, the production of which between August, 1938, and

The occupation of Prague. The loss of Czechoslovakia to the Allies robbed us not only of the line of defences along the Western perimeter, reputed to be nearly as strong as the Maginot Line, but of the first-class Czech Army and the huge Skoda armament factories. *(Radio Times Hulton Picture Library)*

September, 1939, was itself nearly equal to the actual output of British arms factories in that period, was made to change sides adversely.

Oddly enough, this great tide of woes seemed to put a new spirit into the British people. The news was so bad that none of the old attitudes was relevant any more. Peace Pledge Unions and Popular Fronts were now beside the point, like a man on the scaffold deciding to mount a 'No More Hanging' movement. The illusions of the Thirties gradually melted away – and they had been many. In the new cold light the 'committed' could be seen as the self-licensed liars and con-men so many of them had become, whether of Left or Right, whether Hitler's 'new manliness' had held them mesmerised or Stalin's 'workers' paradise'.

The last to go were the illusions about the power of Britain in the world. We might survive, we now knew, and that was all. Conscription came in on 1 July. In August there was a trial black-out and, since the whole world had now gone mad, the Russians signed a non-aggression pact with Germany. If you felt like being funny, it was a bit of a joke to listen to the Communists trying to find something nice to say about their new ally.

The present seemed not to exist, we only had a past and a future. Works of art were being stored in the caves of Derbyshire and the mineshafts of Wales. From Canterbury we evacuated the stained glass and from our great cities the children.

We'd 'bought it' as the phrase then was, and at eleven o'clock on 3 September we heard Mr Chamberlain, speaking in a strained and disgusted voice, tell us that we were at war with Germany. We were surprised how little we felt. A minute later the air-raid siren sounded. It was the last of the Thirties' false alarms.

Overleaf
On 3 September 1939 Chamberlain made his famous broadcast to tell the British nation that it was at war with Germany. An air-raid siren sounded in earnest for the first time, though it was a false alarm; a Royal Proclamation was issued calling up the Reserves and Churchill was at last brought in. *(Radio Times Hulton Picture Library)*

BY THE KING
A PROCLAMATION
SPECIFYING THE ARTICLES TO BE TREATED AS CONTRABAND OF WAR
GEORGE R.I.
BY THE KING
A PROCLAMAT
FOR CONTINUING AIRMEN IN AIR FORCE S
GEORGE R.I.
GOD SAVE THE K
PARTIAL MOB
ROYAL AIR FORC

BY THE KING
A PROCLAMATION
FOR CALLING OUT THE ARMY RESERVE (INCLUDING THE MILITIA) AND
EMBODYING THE TERRITORIAL ARMY
GOD SAVE THE K

BY THE KING
A PROCLAMATION
FOR CALLING OUT THE AIR FORCE RESERVE AND EMBODYING
THE AUXILIARY AIR FORCE
GOD SAVE THE KING

Only the teacher seems anxious, but for hundreds of thousands of city children evacuation to the safety of the country proved a traumatic experience. Labelled like parcels and each carrying a little bundle of possessions, these children were on their way to a totally new way of life. *(Keystone Press Agency Ltd)*

14 · *Afterthoughts*

During the Sixties, although the Thirties generation – now in their fifties – often felt they'd been sitting there so long that the film had come round again, this was only because the young were making a big noise in the world once more and, as usual, it was a paranoid political and philosophical noise. But the differences between the decades were profound. Much the same things got themselves said: I don't think I heard a single 'provocative' statement made in the Sixties which I had not heard before, or used myself in the Thirties, but the swine before whom these pearls were cast were a different breed in a different sty. Mass-man had not arrived in the Thirties, and the life-style of the foetus, protected in the womb of the State from any outside shock, kept at an even temperature and supplied with adequate nourishment, which now seems pretty generally accepted as the high ideal towards which civilisation must make its way, would have seemed unbearable then. How man behaved in masses was of interest only to politicians and advertisers, but each man's particularity – what made him different – was the cultural staple. Fiction was devoted entirely to that subject. Separateness was highly valued. The 'fictionalised' television documentary of today, in which a 'character' concocted from statistics is seen to react to an environment similarly concocted in order to illustrate some social theory of the author, would have seemed, and seems to me, a barbarous piece of insolence. Rousseau's proposition that 'Man is born free and is everywhere in chains' would have received little assent in Britain in the Thirties, when it was assumed that man was born attached to a ball and chain of genetic characteristics, many of them potentially disastrous, from whose ruinous effects only a strong civilised tradition with a trained intellect and possibly, for some people, the grace of God, could redeem him.

The most profound difference was the fact that British culture, as always a literary one, still had a strong grip on British life. Words celebrate differences: differences present choices. The chief concern, certainly of education and probably of life itself, was the making of choices between concepts. Most of the choices had already been made by a long line of intellectuals stretching back to the Greeks and incorporated in the civilised tradition. The process was still going on and was the raison d'etre of the human race. Mr Baldwin, who led us during the Thirties, was an almost comically good example of a product of this culture. Most of the time he dozed in a literary dream: towards anything which seemed to threaten it he could become at once as adroit and ruthless as a gangster. The concept of equality threatened its very roots. Even Auden, who willed 'the death of the old gang', wrote that Time

> 'worships language and forgives
> Everyone by whom it lives.'

That language is now obviously in a poor state of health is the chief difference between then and now. A sociologist can offer an observation: a writer, if he is a good enough one, an experience.

100 Thirties People

Sir John Anderson 1882-1958. Administrator and politician. Governor of Bengal 1932. Home Secretary and Minister of Home Security 1939-40. The Anderson shelter was named after him.
Fred Astaire b 1899. Film actor and dancer. His partnership with Ginger Rogers produced some of the best musical films of the Thirties, including *Roberta* and *The Gay Divorce* in 1935, and *Top Hat* in 1936.
Clement Attlee 1883-1967. Labour statesman. Became deputy leader of the Opposition after the split of 1931, and leader in 1935.
W. H. Auden 1907-73. Poet. Published *Poems* 1930, *The Orators* 1932, *Look, Stranger* 1936 and, with Christopher Isherwood, the plays *The Dog Beneath the Skin* 1935 and *The Ascent of F.6* 1936.
Stanley Baldwin 1867-1947. Conservative statesman. Lord President in 1931 National Government. Prime Minister for the third time 1935-7.
Lord Beaverbrook 1879-1964. Newspaper proprietor and Conservative politician. His main paper, the *Daily Express*, had, by the mid-Thirties, the highest circulation in the world. He used it to campaign for Empire Free Trade, his major obsession.
Sir Thomas Beecham 1879-1961. Conductor. Principal conductor of Covent Garden Opera House 1932. In the same year founded the London Philharmonic Orchestra. Popularised the music of Mozart, Strauss, Delius and Sibelius.
Busby Berkeley b 1895. Hollywood film director. Directed the dance sequences in a number of the most popular musical films of the Thirties, including *The Gold Diggers of 1933*.
Don Bradman b 1908. Australian cricketer, the most brilliant batsman of the Thirties. He played for Australia for twenty years from 1928 and was captain from 1936.
Sir Malcolm Campbell 1885-1949. Record-breaking driver of cars and speed boats. Achieved the world land speed record of 301mph in 1935.
Neville Chamberlain 1869-1940. Conservative statesman. Minister of Health August 1931, Chancellor of the Exchequer November 1931 and 1935, Prime Minister 1937-40.
Charles Chaplin b 1889. Film comedian and director, *City Lights* 1931, *Modern Times* 1936.
Chiang Kai-shek b 1887. Chinese statesman and general. Nationalist leader of China during the Thirties.

Agatha Christie 1890-1976. Novelist. The chief British detective story writer of her age, and creator of Hercule Poirot and Miss Marple.
Winston Churchill 1874-1965. Statesman. In the wings of politics during the Thirties, until recalled to be First Lord of the Admiralty in September 1939.
Charles Cochran 1873-1951. Impresario. Staged *Cochran's Revues* of 1930 and 1931, Noel Coward's *Cavalcade* 1931. Famous for his team of highly trained chorus girls 'Mr Cochran's Young Ladies'.
William Coldstream b 1908. Painter. In association with Claude Rogers and Victor Pasmore, he founded the Euston Road School of Painting in 1937.
Noel Coward 1899-1973. Actor, playwright and composer. *Private Lives* 1930, *Cavalcade* 1931, *Words and Music* 1932, *Design for Living* 1932, *Tonight at 8.30* 1935.
Sir Stafford Cripps 1889-1952. Labour politician. Leader of the Socialist League 1931. Expelled from the Labour Party in 1939 for his support of the Popular Front.
Salvador Dali b 1904. Spanish painter, and propagandist for the Surrealist movement. His best work was done during the Thirties.
Walt Disney 1901-66. American film cartoonist. His *Silly Symphonies* were extremely popular, and his first full-length film *Snow White and the Seven Dwarfs* was the great hit of 1938 in Britain.
Eamon de Valera 1882-1975. Irish Statesman. Leader of the Opposition in the Irish Free State Parliament 1927-32. President of the Executive Council of the Irish Free State Parliament and Minister for External Affairs 1932-7. Became head of the government of Eire after the 1937 constitution.
Robert Donat 1905-58. Film actor. *The Private Life of Henry VIII* 1932, *The Count of Monte Cristo* 1934, *The Thirty-nine Steps* 1935, *Goodbye Mr Chips* 1939.
Alfred Duff Cooper 1890-1954. Conservative politician. Secretary for War 1935-7. First Lord of the Admiralty 1938. Resigned in protest against the Munich agreement.
Anthony Eden b 1897. Conservative politician. Under-Secretary for Foreign Affairs 1931, Lord Privy Seal 1934, Foreign Secretary 1935. Resigned 1938 in protest against Chamberlain's personal intervention in negotiations with Mussolini.
T. S. Eliot 1888-1965. Poet and critic. During the Thirties much concerned with poetic drama. Edited the *Criterion* until 1939. *Murder in the Cathedral* (play) 1935, *The Use of Poetry and the Use of Criticism* 1933, *Collected Poems 1909-1935* 1936, *The Family Reunion* (play) 1939.
Jacob Epstein 1880-1959. Sculptor whose large allegorical carved figures, in the idiom of primitive sculpture, caused a sensation in the Thirties. *Genesis* 1930, *Ecce Homo* 1934, *Consummatum Est* 1937, *Adam* 1938.
Gracie Fields b 1898. Singer and comedienne, at the peak of her popularity during the Thirties. *Sally in Our Alley* 1932

General Franco 1892-1975. Spanish dictator. Led the army rebellion against the Spanish government in 1936, and by 1937 was political as well as military ruler of Nationalist Spain.
Sigmund Freud 1856-1939. Austrian psychoanalyst. His concept of the unconscious mind is at the root of much of the intellectual development of the Thirties. Settled in London after the invasion of Austria by Nazi Germany.
Mahatma Gandhi 1869-1948. Indian leader, the moving spirit of the civil disobedience campaigns of 1930 and 1932. Came to London 1931 for the second session of the Round Table Conference. Imprisoned in 1932, and undertook 'fast unto death'. Resigned from Congress 1934, but continued to be the major influence in the Indian independence campaign.
Greta Garbo b 1905. Major Hollywood star throughout the Thirties. *Queen Christina* 1934, *Anna Karenina* 1935, *Camille* 1937, *Ninotchka* 1939.
John Gielgud b 1904. Actor and producer. *The Good Companions* 1931, *Richard of Bordeaux* 1932.
Josef Goebbels 1897-1945. Nazi propagandist. In 1933 became Hitler's Minister for Propaganda and Social Enlightenment. Organised the great Nazi rallies, and was responsible for censorship of press, film and radio.
Hermann Goering 1893-1946. Nazi politician. President of the Reichstag 1932. Police chief of Prussia 1933. Created the Luftwaffe, and was in charge of the Four Year Plan.
Victor Gollancz 1893-1967. Publisher. Founded the Left Book Club 1936.
Robert Graves b. 1895. Poet and novelist. *Collected Poems* 1938. *I, Claudius* (novel) 1934.
Graham Greene b 1904. Novelist. *Stamboul Train* 1932, *England Made Me* 1935, *A Gun for Sale* 1936, *Brighton Rock* 1938.
Lord Halifax 1881-1959. Conservative statesman. Viceroy of India 1926-31, Foreign Secretary 1938-40.
Tom Harrisson 1911-76. Anthropologist. Founded Mass Observation with Charles Madge 1936. *Mass Observation* 1937.
Basil Liddell Hart 1895-1970. Writer on military theory, and advocate of the use of mobile armoured formations.
Barbara Hepworth 1903-75. One of the leading non-figurative sculptors working in Britain during the Thirties. Married to Ben Nicholson until 1951.
Heinrich Himmler 1900-45. Nazi police chief. Head of the SS and the Gestapo.
Adolf Hitler 1889-1945. Nazi dictator. Came to power in Germany in 1933, with the support of Nazi, Nationalist and Centre parties, and proceeded to carry out systematically the policies he had earlier outlined in *Mein Kampf*. He took Germany out of the League of Nations and the Disarmament Conference (October 1933) and introduced conscription in March 1935. His naval treaty with Britain in June 1935 put paid to the Versailles Treaty. In March 1936 his troops re-entered

the Rhineland. The Rome-Berlin Axis in 1936 reinforced his alliance with Italy and simplified the annexation of Austria in 1938, and the Munich agreement in September 1938 delivered Czechoslovakia into his hands. Finally, the Non-Aggression Pact with his natural adversary, the Soviet Union, signed in August 1939, bought him time to invade Poland on 1 September. His seven years clear run in Europe was not checked until Britain and France declared war on 3 September 1939.
Sir Samuel Hoare 1880-1959. Conservative politician. Secretary of state for India 1931-5. Foreign Secretary 1935. Resigned over the Hoare-Laval pact December 1935. First Lord of the Admiralty 1936. Home Secretary 1937-9. Lord Privy Seal September 1939.
Jack Hobbs 1882-1963. Cricketer. In the early Thirties still the supreme English batsman of his time. He did not retire until 1934.
Leslie Hore-Belisha 1893-1957. Politician. First Chairman of the National Liberal Party 1931. Minister of Transport 1934. Introduced the Highway Code, driving tests and belisha beacons. Secretary of State for War 1937-40.
Leslie Howard 1893-1959. Actor, producer and film director. Films include *Berkeley Square* 1933, *The Scarlet Pimpernel* 1934, *Pygmalion* 1938 and *Gone with the Wind* 1939.
Aldous Huxley 1894-1963. Novelist. *Brave New World* 1932, *Eyeless in Gaza* 1936, *After Many a Summer* 1939.
Augustus John 1878-1961. Painter. Despite the bravura of his style, both in his work and in his life, he became a fashionable portrait painter during the Thirties. He resigned from the Royal Academy in 1938.
Amy Johnson 1903-41. Aviator. Flew solo from London to Australia in 20 days in 1930.
James Joyce 1882-1941. Irish novelist. *Ulysses*, first published abroad in 1922, was banned in Britain until 1936. *Finnegan's Wake* 1939.
Carl Jung 1876-1961. Psychologist and philosopher. The priest of the collective unconscious, and inventor of the terms 'extrovert and 'introvert'.
McKnight Kauffer 1890-1954. American-born graphic artist. During the Thirties, he designed posters for London Transport and for Shell.
John Maynard Keynes 1883-1946. Economist, who advocated increased government investment to create employment as an answer to depression. *A Treatise on Money* 1930, *General Theory of Employment, Interest and Money* 1936.
Alexander Korda 1893-1956. Film producer. Came to Britain from Hollywood, and in 1932 founded Denham Studios. Films *The Private Life of Henry VIII* 1934, *Rembrandt* 1936, *Things to Come* 1936.
George Lansbury 1859-1940. Labour politician and pacifist. First Commissioner of Works 1929-31. Established Hyde Park Lido. Leader of the Labour Party 1931-5. Resigned over League of Nations sanctions.
Stan Laurel 1890-1965 and **Oliver Hardy** 1892-1957. US film comedians, very popular in this country in the Thirties. Their partnership began in 1926 and went on until 1953.

D. H. Lawrence 1885-1930. Novelist and poet. *Lady Chatterley's Lover* 1928 was banned in Britain until 1960. His influence continued to grow during the decade following his death.
Cecil Day Lewis 1904-72. Poet. Left Communist Party 1939. *From Feathers to Iron* 1931, *Collected Poems* 1935, *Overtures to Death* 1938.
Wyndham Lewis 1884-1957. Artist, writer and critic. Founded *Blast*, the Vorticist magazine, with Ezra Pound. *Men Without Art* 1934, *Blasting and Bombardiering* 1937.
David Lloyd George 1863-1945. Statesman. The former Liberal Prime Minister was in retirement at Churt during most of the Thirties, writing his memoirs. He launched the unsuccessful Council for Action for Peace and Reconstruction in 1935. After a visit to Hitler in 1936, he attacked appeasement and urged cooperation with Russia.
David Low 1891-1963. Cartoonist, creator of Colonel Blimp and the TUC carthorse. Despite his Left-wing sympathies, Low did his best work for the Beaverbrook press.
Ramsay MacDonald 1866-1937. Statesman. Labour Party leader 1922-31. Prime Minister 1929-31 (Second Labour Government) and 1931-5 (National Government).
Louis MacNeice 1907-63. Poet and writer. Often linked with Auden and Spender, but politically less committed to the extreme Left. *Poems* 1935, *The Earth Compels* 1938, *Autumn Journal* 1939.
Stanley Matthews b 1915. Footballer, the best known and respected of the decade. First played for England at the age of twenty, and thereafter scarcely put a foot wrong.
Henry Moore b 1898. Sculptor. Exhibited in London throughout the Thirties, but his work was not yet widely known outside art circles.
Oswald Mosley b 1896. Politician. Originally a Conservative, he held office in the 1929 Labour Government, but left the Labour Party 1930 to found the New Party. In 1932 he founded the British Union of Fascists.
Benito Mussolini 1883-1945. Italian dictator. In power since 1922. His close relationship with Hitler was formalised by the Rome-Berlin Axis of 1936. Invaded Abyssinia 1936 and Albania 1939.
Ben Nicholson b 1894. Painter. One of the few British painters with an international reputation in the Thirties. Influenced by Mondrian, Braque and Picasso.
Lord Nuffield 1877-1963. Pioneer motor manufacturer who, with his Morris and MG cars, did for the British motor industry what Ford did for the American.
George Orwell (Eric Blair) 1903-50. Novelist and writer. *Down and Out in Paris and London* 1933, *Burmese Days* 1935, *The Road to Wigan Pier* 1937, *Homage to Catalonia* 1938, *Coming Up for Air* 1939.
Jesse Owens b 1913. American negro athlete. Won 3 individual gold medals, and one team gold medal, at the 1936 Olympic Games.
Pablo Picasso 1881-1973. Spanish painter. Haunted during the Thirties by the images of the weeping woman and the dying horse, and by a vision of the horrors of war. 'Guernica' 1937 was the picture that took

most powerful hold of the public imagination. 'Night Fishing at Antibes' 1939.
J. B. Priestley b 1894. Novelist and playwright. Books *The Good Companions* 1929, *Angel Pavement* 1930, *English Journey* 1934. Plays *The Good Companions* 1931, *Laburnum Grove* 1933, *Time and the Conways* 1937
John Reith 1889-1971. Director General of the British Broadcasting Corporation 1927-38.
J. von Ribbentrop 1893-1946. German diplomat. Joined Nazi Party 1932. Special envoy on disarmament 1934-6. Ambassador to London 1936-8.
Franklin D. Roosevelt 1882-1945. President of the United States 1933-45. His 'New Deal' policy initiated the recovery of the American economy from the depression.
Sir Walter Runciman 1870-1949. Liberal and, later, Liberal National politician. President of the Board of Trade 1931-7. Lord President of the Council 1938-9.
Bertrand Russell 1872-1970. Philosopher and mathematician. His influence, particularly in matters of education and pacifism, was important for Left-wing intellectuals during the Thirties. *Education and the Social Order* 1932, *Marriage and Morals* 1932.
Bernard Shaw 1856-1950. Playwright. By the Thirties most of his work lay behind him, but he remained well in the public eye as a Grand Old Man. Visited Russia 1931. *The Black Girl in Search of God* 1932, *Too True to be Good* 1932.
R. C. Sherriff 1896-1975. Playwright. *Journey's End* 1929. Wrote the script for the films *The Invisible Man* 1933 and *Goodbye Mr Chips* 1936.
Sir John Simon 1873-1954. Liberal politician. Foreign Secretary 1931. Leader of the National Liberal Party 1931. Home Secretary 1935-7. Chancellor of the Exchequer 1937-40.
Philip Snowden 1864-1937. Labour politician. Chancellor of the Exchequer 1929-31. Remained in the National Government from a sense of duty. Lord Privy Seal 1931, but resigned over preferential tariffs 1932.
Stanley Spencer 1891-1959. Painter. His paintings of Biblical subjects in modern contexts were well known to the public. His resignation from the Royal Academy when two of his works were rejected created a minor sensation.
Stephen Spender b 1909. Poet and critic, often linked in the public mind with Auden and MacNeice. *Twenty Poems* 1930, *Poems from Spain* 1939.
Josef Stalin 1879-1953. Russian leader, in control after 1927. In Russia the decade was marked by drastic purges and very poor living standards, but considerable industrial development. Stalin gave support to the Government side in the Spanish Civil War, but did not commit himself too deeply. Negotiated with Britain after Munich, but finally signed a non-aggression pact with Hitler in August 1939.
John Strachey 1901-63. Politician, influenced by Marxist theory.

Resigned from the Labour Party 1931. Wrote *The Menace of Fascism* 1933, *The Theory and Practice of Socialism* 1936.

Graham Sutherland b 1903. Painter. Originally specialised in etching, but during the Thirties turned to painting, mainly abstract but romantic landscapes.

Richard Tauber 1891-1948. Austrian-born tenor. Brought *The Land of Smiles* to London in 1931. Appeared at Covent Garden 1938.

Shirley Temple b 1928. From 1934 to 1939 the most successful of all the Hollywood child stars. Her films included *Rebecca of Sunnybrook Farm* and *Wee Willie Winkie*.

Ralph Vaughan Williams 1872-1958. Composer. 'Magnificat' 1932, Fourth Symphony 1935. Awarded Order of Merit 1935.

Evelyn Waugh 1903-66. Novelist. *Vile Bodies* 1930, *Black Mischief* 1932, *A Handful of Dust* 1934, *Scoop* 1938.

H. G. Wells 1866-1946. Writer. His most prolific period was over by the Thirties, but *The Science of Life* which he produced with Julian Huxley and G. P. Wells in 1929-30 was proof of his undiminished intellectual range. His *Experiment in Autobiography* appeared in 1934.

Ellen Wilkinson 1891-1947. Labour politician and MP for Jarrow 1935. The moving spirit behind the Jarrow Crusade.

P. G. Wodehouse 1881-1975. Writer. Creator of Bertie Wooster and Jeeves. *Right Ho, Jeeves* 1934, *Blandings Castle* 1935, *Summer Moonshine* 1938.

Sir Henry Wood 1869-1944. Conductor. Throughout the Thirties he was conducting the Promenade Concerts at the Queen's Hall.

Virginia Woolf 1882-1941. Novelist and critic. *The Waves* 1931, *The Years* 1937.

W. B. Yeats 1865-1939. Irish poet and playwright. Yeats produced some of his best work in the last years of his life. His *Collected Poems* were published in 1933.

Events and Entertainments of the Year

1930

Politics

Second Reparation Conference at The Hague – German Reparations set at 38 milliard gold marks over 59 years (3-30 Jan).
Gandhi began Indian civil disobedience campaign (12 March).
Haile Selassie became Emperor of Abyssinia (3 Apr).
The Allied occupation of Germany ended (30 June).
107 Nazis returned in German elections (14 Sept).
Round Table Conference on India held in London (12 Nov-19 Jan).

General

Perspex invented.
D. H. Lawrence died.
France began to build the Maginot Line.

Sport

Youth Hostels Association founded.
Women's League of Health and Beauty started.
Amy Johnson's solo flight to Australia.
Mixed bathing began at the Serpentine.
Don Bradman first played for Australia in England.
The first British Empire Games were held in Canada.
Popular crazes for 'yo-yo' and midget golf began.

Stage

The Barretts of Wimpole Street.
Cochran's 1930 Review.
Private Lives with Gertrude Laurence and Noel Coward.
Hamlet with John Gielgud.

Films

The Love Parade with Maurice Chevalier and Jeanette MacDonald.
All Quiet on the Western Front.
Journey's End.
Disraeli with George Arliss.

Hell's Angels with Jean Harlow.

Music

Gigli's debut at Covent Garden.
Elgar's 'Pomp and Circumstance March'.
Delius 3rd Violin Concerto.
Arnold Bax's 2nd and 3rd Symphonies.
Toscanini visited London with the New York Philharmonic Orchestra.
BBC Symphony Orchestra started.

Popular Songs

'On the Sunny Side of the Street'.
'St James Infirmary'.
'Amy, Wonderful Amy'.
'Sleepy Lagoon'.
'Someday I'll Find You'.
'Happy Days Are Here Again'.
'Tiptoe through the Tulips'.

1931

Politics

End of Indian Civil Disobedience campaign (4 March).
Failure of Austrian Kredit Anstalt Bank (11 May).
MacDonald's first National Government formed (25 Aug).
Second India Conference in London, with Gandhi present (7 Sept-1 Dec).
Naval mutiny at Invergordon (15 Sept).
Japanese troops invaded Manchuria (18 Sept).
Britain went off the gold standard (21 Sept).
MacDonald's second National Government formed (5 Nov).
Mosley left Labour Party and formed the New Party.

General

Means test introduced.
Arnold Bennett died.
Whipsnade Zoo opened.

Sport

Schneider Trophy won for Britain for the third time.

Stage

The White Horse Inn.
Cavalcade by Noel Coward.
Autumn Crocus by Dodie Smith.
The Good Companions by J. B. Priestley and E. Knoblock.
The Anatomist by James Bridie.

Films
Flowers and Trees, Disney's first technicolour cartoon.
City Lights with Charlie Chaplin.
The Blue Angel with Marlene Dietrich.

Music
Walton's *Belshazzar's Feast* performed at Leeds.
Paderewski concert at the Albert Hall.
Richard Strauss and Igor Stravinski visited London.
Season of Russian opera and ballet at the Lyceum Theatre.

Art
Epstein and Moore both exhibited at the Leicester Galleries, London.

Popular Songs
'Goodnight, Sweetheart'.
'Sally'.
'You are my Heart's Delight'.
'Life is Just a Bowl of Cherries'.
'I'm Happy when I'm Hiking'.

1932

Politics
Gandhi arrested, and special powers given to Indian Government for six months (4 Jan).
Disarmament Conference began at Geneva (2 Feb).
De Valera became Irish Prime Minister (9 March).
Reparation Conference at Lausanne – Germany agreed final provisional payment of 3 milliard marks (16 June-9 July).
Anglo-French pact of friendship signed at Lausanne (13 July).
Imperial Economic Conference held at Ottawa (21 July-20 Aug).
196 Nazis returned in German elections (6 Nov).
Roosevelt elected President of USA (8 Nov).
Third India Conference in London (19 Nov-24 Dec).
Sir Oswald Mosley founded British Union of Fascists.

General
Piccadilly Circus first lit by electricity.
BBC moved from Savoy Hill to Broadcasting House.
Unemployed Hunger March to London.
First Christmas Day broadcast by King George V.
Shakespeare Memorial Theatre at Stratford-on-Avon opened.
BBC Empire Service began.
Henry Hall's BBC Dance Orchestra succeeded Jack Payne's.
Galsworthy awarded Nobel Prize for literature.
Lytton Strachey and Edgar Wallace died.

Sport
First test matches between England and India.

Stage
While Parents Sleep by Anthony Kimmins.
The Cat and the Fiddle with music by Jerome Kern.
Words and Music by Noel Coward.
Dangerous Corner by J. B. Priestley.

Films
Sally in Our Alley with Gracie Fields.
The Ghost Train with Cicely Courtneidge and Jack Hulbert.
Goodnight Vienna with Jack Buchanan.

Music
The London Philharmonic Orchestra founded by Sir Thomas Beecham.

Popular Songs
'Mad about the Boy'.
'Ain't it Grand to be Blooming Well Dead'.
'Brother, Can You Spare a Dime?'
'Night and Day'.
'Shuffle off to Buffalo'.

1933

Politics
Hitler became Reich Chancellor (30 Jan).
Reichstag Fire (27 Feb).
Roosevelt inaugurated the New Deal (March).
Japan left the League of Nations (27 March).
Anglo-German trade pact (27 Apr).
USA went off the gold standard (30 Apr).
Truce between China and Japan, leaving Japan in occupation of China north of the Great Wall (31 May).
World Economic Conference held in London (12 June-27 July).
Political parties, other than Nazis, banned in Germany (14 July).
Four-Power Pact (Britain, France, Germany and Italy) signed (15 July).
Germany left League of Nations and Disarmament Conference (14 Oct).

General
Unemployment in Britain reached its peak of just under 3 million in January.
London Passenger Transport Board founded.
Oxford Union 'King and Country' resolution.

Polythene first made.
Prohibition ended in America.
Loch Ness monster sensation.
The first woman announcer employed by the BBC.
In Town Tonight began on radio.
John Galsworthy died.

Sport
Cricket 'Bodyline' bowling row.
The Davis Cup for tennis won by Britain.

Stage
Richard of Bordeaux with John Gielgud.
Ten Minute Alibi by Anthony Armstrong.
Escape Me Never with Elizabeth Bergner.
Laburnum Grove by J. B. Priestley.
The Wind and the Rain.
The Gay Divorce with music by Cole Porter.

Films
Cavalcade with Diana Wynyard and Clive Brook.
Grand Hotel with Greta Garbo.
The Good Companions with Jessie Matthews and John Gielgud.
The Sign of the Cross with Charles Laughton and Frederick Marsh.
She Done Him Wrong with Mae West.
The Face of Britain (documentary) by Paul Rotha.
King Kong.

Music
Constant Lambert's Piano Concerto.
The Ballets Russes of Monte Carlo played a season in London.

Popular Songs
'Teddy Bears' Picnic'.
'There's Something about a Soldier'.
'Who's Afraid of the Big, Bad Wolf?'.

1934

Politics
Gandhi suspended civil disobedience campaign in India (7 Apr).
Hitler and Mussolini met in Venice (14-15 June).
Nazi purge in Germany – 'The Night of the Long Knives' (30 June).
Nazi revolt in Austria – murder of Dollfuss (25 July).
Hindenburg died and Hitler became Führer (19 Aug).
Russia joined League of Nations (18 Sept).

General

British 'peace ballot' organised by the League of Nations Union.
Liner *Queen Mary* launched.
Ministry of Transport introduced new road signs and belisha beacons.
The Betting and Lotteries Act – greyhound tracks licensed, the totalisator allowed, but lotteries made illegal.

Stage

The Moon in the Yellow River by Denis Johnston.
Conversation Piece by Noel Coward.
Eden End by J. B. Priestley.

Films

The Private Life of Henry VIII with Charles Laughton.
The Emperor Jones with Paul Robeson.
The Thin Man with Myrna Loy and William Powell.
The Barretts of Wimpole Street with Norma Shearer and Charles Laughton.
Evergreen with Jessie Matthews.
Duck Soup with the Marx Brothers.
Queen Christina with Greta Garbo.
Nell Gwyn with Anna Neagle.

Music

Elgar, Holst and Delius died.
Sir Walford Davies succeeded Sir Edward Elgar as Master of the King's Musick.

Popular Songs

'Isle of Capri'.
'I'll Follow My Secret Heart'.
'Ole Faithful'.
'With Her Head Tucked Underneath Her Arm'.
'Smoke Gets in Your Eyes'.

1935

Politics

After January plebiscite, Saar returned to Germany (7 March).
Germany repudiated the military provisions of the Treaty of Versailles (16 March).
Baldwin became Prime Minister of National Government (7 June).
Anglo-German Naval Agreement (18 June).
Government of India Act passed (2 Aug).
Nuremberg Laws outlawed Jews in Germany (15 Sept).
Mussolini invaded Abyssinia (2 Oct).
Baldwin Government returned in General Election (Nov).

League of Nations instituted economic sanctions against Italy (18 Nov).
Chiang Kai-shek elected President of Chinese Executive (1 Dec).
Hoare-Laval pact and subsequent public outcry (December).
Anthony Eden succeeded Sir Samuel Hoare as Foreign Secretary (18 Dec).

General

Silver Jubilee of King George V and Queen Mary.
Penguin Books founded.
Watson-Watt invented Radar.
Unemployment dropped below two million in August.
Peace Pledge Union started.
Air Raid Precautions instituted by the Home Office.

Stage

Night Must Fall with Emlyn Williams.
Love on the Dole with Wendy Hiller.
1066 and All That.
Romeo and Juliet with Peggy Ashcroft and John Gielgud.
Murder in the Cathedral by T. S. Eliot.
Glamorous Night with Ivor Novello.
Anything Goes with music by Cole Porter.

Films

Clive of India with Ronald Colman.
Sanders of the River with Paul Robeson and Leslie Banks.
David Copperfield with Freddie Bartholomew.
Roberta and *The Gay Divorce* with Fred Astaire and Ginger Rogers.
The Thirty-nine Steps with Robert Donat.
The Scarlet Pimpernel with Leslie Howard and Merle Oberon.
Micky Mouse appeared in colour for the first time.

Music

William Walton's First Symphony.

Art

Chinese Exhibition at Burlington House.

Popular Songs

'Red Sails in the Sunset'.
'Why Did She Fall for the Leader of the Band'.
'Dinner for One, Please, James'.
'On the Good Ship Lollipop'.
'Anything Goes'.

1936

Politics

George V died (20 Jan) and was succeeded by Edward VIII.
Victory for Popular Front in the Spanish Elections (16 Feb).
Germany reoccupied the Rhineland (7 March).
London Naval Pact between Britain, France and USA (25 March).
Haile Selassie left Abyssinia (1 May).
Army rebellion began the Spanish Civil War (18 July).
Germany introduced conscription (24 Aug).
Non-Intervention Committee met in London (9 Sept).
The 'Jarrow crusade' (5 Oct).
The Rome-Berlin Axis proclaimed by Mussolini (1 Nov).
Germany and Italy recognised Franco (18 Nov).
Abdication of Edward VIII (10 Dec) and succession of George VI (11 Dec).

General

Crystal Palace destroyed by fire.
BBC Television started transmission from Alexandra Palace.
Millionth telephone installation in the London area.
First Butlin Holiday Camp opened at Skegness.
London-Paris train ferry service started.

Sport

Olympic Games held in Berlin.
Fred Perry was Wimbledon tennis champion for the third year in succession.

Stage

French Without Tears by Terence Rattigan.
Careless Rapture by Noel Coward.
Storm in a Teacup by James Bridie.
Tonight at 8.30 by Noel Coward.

Films

Mr Deeds Goes to Town with Gary Cooper.
Modern Times by Chaplin.
Things to Come.
The Great Ziegfeld with William Powell and Myrna Loy.

Art

Exhibition of Surrealist Art at the New Burlington Galleries.

Popular Songs

'These Foolish Things'.
'Did Your Mother Come from Ireland'.

'The Fleet's in Port Again'.
'The Touch of Your Lips'.

1937

Politics

Imperial Conference in London (14 May-15 June).
Germany and Italy left Non-Intervention Committee (23 June).
Baldwin succeeded as Prime Minister by Neville Chamberlain (28 June).
Japan attacked China (7 July).
Rioting in Sudetenland (17 Oct).
Italy joined Germany and Japan in the Anti-Comintern Pact (6 Nov).
Lord Halifax visited Hitler (17-21 Nov).

General

Coronation of King George VI.
Paris World Fair.
ARP duties imposed on local authorities.
A. P. Herbert's Divorce Bill extended grounds for divorce.

Stage

French Without Tears by Terence Rattigan.
Me and My Girl with Flanagan and Allen.
Time and the Conways by J. B. Priestley.
Mourning Becomes Electra by Eugene O'Neill.
Victoria Regina by Laurence Housman.
The Ascent of F.6 by Auden and Isherwood.

Films

Three Smart Girls with Deanna Durbin.
Show Boat with Paul Robeson.
Oh, Mr Porter with Will Hay.
Lost Horizon with Ronald Colman.
Camille with Greta Garbo.

Music

Toscanini conducted the BBC Orchestra in eight concerts.

Popular Songs

'Leaning on a Lamppost'.
'Walter, Lead me to the Altar'.
'She's My Lovely'.
'A Nice Cup of Tea'.
'I've Got You Under My Skin'.

1938

Politics

Hitler assumed supreme command (4 Feb).
Anthony Eden resigned as Foreign Secretary (20 Feb).
Lord Halifax became Foreign Secretary (25 Feb).
Austria annexed by Germany (12 March).
Agreement between Britain and Eire signed (25 Apr).
Hitler and Mussolini met in Rome (3-9 May).

German mobilisation (12 Aug).
Chamberlain met Hitler at Berchtesgaden (15 Sept), Godesberg (22 Sept) and Munich (29 Sept).
The Munich Agreement between Britain, France, Germany and Italy (29 Sept).

General

First British National Register for war service prepared.
New York World Fair.
Liner *Queen Elizabeth* launched.
Nylon first produced.
Picture Post first published.
400,000 steel Anderson shelters manufactured for civilian use.
Women's Voluntary Service and Women's Auxiliary Territorial Force founded.
BBC began broadcasts to foreign countries.
Empire Exhibition at Glasgow.
Holidays with Pay Act passed.
BBC comedy series *Band Wagon* began.

Sport

England made record cricket score of 903 for seven wickets against Australia.

Stage

The Corn is Green by Emlyn Williams
The Flashing Stream by Charles Morgan.
Idiot's Delight by Robert Sherwood.
Dear Octopus by Dodie Smith.
Operette by Noel Coward.

Films

Snow White and the Seven Dwarfs by Disney.
The Prisoner of Zenda with Ronald Colman.
Sixty Glorious Years with Anna Neagle.
The Good Earth with Paul Muni.
The Lady Vanishes directed by Hitchcock.

Music

Sibelius Festival, directed by Sir Thomas Beecham, held in London.
John McCormack gave his final recital.
The Berlin Philharmonic orchestra, under Fürtwangler, and the Prague Philharmonic Orchestra, under Kubelik, visited Britain.

Popular Songs

'Blue Skies are round the Corner'.
'I'll Walk Beside You'.
'Little Drummer Boy'.
'The Lambeth Walk'.
'Music, Maestro, Please'.
'Whistle While You Work'.

1939

Politics

Britain recognised Franco regime in Spain (28 Feb).
German troops invaded Czechoslovakia (15 March).
British guarantee given to Poland (24 March).
Italy invaded Albania (7 Apr).
Russia proposed alliance with Britain and France (16 Apr).
Call-up of men of 20 and 21 for military training announced (26 Apr).
German-Italian ten year alliance (22 May).
Ministry of Supply set up (11 July).
Trial black-out over half Britain (23 Aug).
Non-Aggression Pact between Germany and Russia (23 Aug).
Emergency Powers Bill rushed through Parliament (24 Aug).
Anglo-Polish Mutual Assistance Pact (25 Aug).
German ultimatum to Poland (29 Aug).
Black-out began in Britain (1 Sept).
Britain, France, Australia and New Zealand declared war on Germany (3 Sept).
Chamberlain's War Cabinet formed, with Churchill as First Lord of the Admiralty (3 Sept).
Russia invaded Poland (17 Sept) and Finland (30 Nov).

General

First Anderson shelters distributed in London on 25 February.
Women's Auxiliary Air Force and Women's Royal Naval Service set up.
First broadcast of *ITMA*.
National Identity cards introduced (abolished 1952).

Sport

Sir Malcolm Campbell achieved world water speed record of 141.74mph

Stage

Johnson over Jordan by J. B. Priestley.
The Family Reunion by T. S. Eliot.
The Dancing Years by Ivor Novello.
Of Mice and Men by John Steinbeck.
The Women by Claire Boothe.

Films

The Citadel with Robert Donat and Ralph Richardson.
Pygmalion with Wendy Hiller and Leslie Howard.
Dark Victory with Bette Davis.
Wuthering Heights with Laurence Olivier and Merle Oberon.
Pinocchio by Disney.
The Lion Has Wings with Ralph Richardson.

Music

Myra Hess started Lunchtime Concerts at the National Gallery.

Popular Songs

'Begin the Beguine .
'Run Rabbit Run'.
'South of the Border'.
'Wish me Luck as You Wave me Goodbye'.
'We'll Meet Again'.
'There'll Always Be an England'.

Further Reading

Baily, Leslie. *Leslie Baily's BBC Scrapbooks, Volume 2 1918-1939* (Allen & Unwin, 1968)
Briggs, Asa. *The History of Broadcasting in the United Kingdom* (Oxford University Press, 1961)
—. *They Saw It Happen* (Blackwell, 1973)
Graves, Robert and Hodge, Alan. *The Long Week-end* (Penguin, 1971)
Laver, James. *Between the Wars*
Mowat, C. L. *Britain between the Wars* (Methuen, 1968)
Muggeridge, Malcolm. *The Thirties* (Fontana, 1971)
Nicholson, Harold. *King George V* (Constable) Jonathan Cape Ltd
Orwell, George. *The Road to Wigan Pier* (Penguin, 1970)
Priestley, J. B. *English Journey* (Heinemann, 1934)
Seaman, L. C. B. *Life in Britain between the Wars* (Batsford, 1970)
Smith, Godfrey (ed). *1000 Makers of the Twentieth Century* (David & Charles, 1972)
Taylor, A. J. P. *English History 1914-1945* (Penguin, 1970)

Acknowledgments

I am most grateful for permission to reproduce quotations from the following works:

The Glory of Parliament by H. Boardman, published by George Allen and Unwin Ltd.

Berlin, the Eagle and the Bear by John Mander, published by Barrie and Rockliff (1959).

'Newsreel' from *Overtures to Death* by Cecil Day Lewis, published by Jonathan Cape Limited and the Hogarth Press.

The Second World War by Winston S. Churchill, published by Cassell & Co., Ltd. (1948-54). Published in USA by Houghton Mifflin Company.

'Epistle I' from *Collected Poems 1930-1955* by George Barker, published by Faber & Faber.

'Consider' from *Collected Shorter Poems* by W. H. Auden, published by Faber & Faber.

'An Eclogue for Christmas' from *Collected Poems of Louis MacNeice*, published by Faber & Faber.

The Life of Neville Chamberlain by Sir Keith Feiling, published by Macmillan London and Basingstoke.

for help in the selection of material for this book, and to Mrs Kathleen Smith for assistance with the manuscript.

Index

Abdication crisis, 104-7
Abyssinian War, 95-100, 117
Aldington, Richard, 9
Amery, Leo, 117
Anschluss, the, 117-18, 120
Askey, Arthur, 78
Astaire, Fred, 79, 80, 81
Attlee, Clement, 113
Auden, W. H., 40, 43, 44, 49, 112, 132
Austin, Bunny, 74, 85, 88

Baer, Max, 86
Baily, Leslie, 77
Baldwin, Stanley, 15, 23, 38-9, 59-61, 69, 95, 100, 106, 115-16, 117, 132
Bank of England, 12-13, 16
Barker, George, 14
Bartlett, Vernon, 93
Bauhaus, the, 56
BBC (British Broadcasting Corporation), 26, 76-8, 102
Beaverbrook, Lord, 107
Bell, Clive, 47
Belloc, Hilaire, 61
Benes, President, 121
Bennett, Arnold, 92
Betjeman, John, 56
Boult, Adrian, 77
Boxing, 86
Bradford, Bishop of, 106-7
Bradman, Don, 86
Branker, Sir Sefton, 84
Braque, 48
Brittain, Vera, 93
Brook, Clive, 80
Buchman, John, 74
Budge, Donald, 88

Campbell, Sir Malcolm, 87
Carnera, Primo, 86
Chamberlain, Neville, 23, 115-17, 118-22, 123, 127
Chaplin, Charles, 80
Chapman, A. P. F., 85
Chirico, 48
Christie, Agatha, 89
Churchill, Winston, 17, 45, 61, 107, 117, 118, 123-7
Cinema, *see also* Hollywood, 21, 78-83
Clapham and Dwyer, 78
Class distinctions, 7-8, 25-6, 28, 30, 34-9, 75
Clothes, 28-38, 46, 88
Cobham, Sir Alan, 83
Cockburn, Claude, 112
Coldstream, William, 49
Colman, Ronald, 28, 81
Communism, *see also* Marxism, 21, 43, 44, 65, 112, 127
Community singing, 73
Conservative Party, 12, 17, 61, 116-17
Constanduros, Mabel, 78
Cooper, Alfred Duff, 107, 115, 117
Cooper, Gary, 80
Cooper, Gladys, 93
Corbusier, Le, 58
Cotton, T. H., 88
Coward, Noel, 38, 77, 93
Cricket, 85-6
Crosby, Bing, 78, 82
Czechoslovakia, 118-21, 123-7

Dali, Salvador, 108-9
Day Lewis, Cecil, 40, 43, 82-3, 112
Depression, the, 12-21, 108

Diaghilev Ballet, 11
Disney, Walt, 82
Dole, the, 17-20, 69
Domestic servants, 21-2
Donat, Robert, 80
Douglas, J. W. H. T., 85

Eden, Anthony, 99, 117
Edward VIII, *see also* Prince of Wale and Duke of Windsor, 102-7
Eliot, T. S., 89, 91
Elizabeth, Princess, 105, 107
Elizabeth, Queen, 105, 107
Empire, the British, 38-9, 76, 85, 102
Epstein, Jacob, 50
Expressionism, 49

Fascists, British Union of (Blackshirts) 62, 69-72, 107
Fields, Gracie, 78, 79, 80, 84
Flanagan and Allen, 78
Foort, Reginald, 78
Football, Association, 85
Formby, George, 79, 80
Forster, E. M., 10
Franco, General, 110, 112-13, 114
Frankau, Ronald, 78
Freud, Sigmund, 46, 105, 108
Furness, Lady, 105

Gable, Clark, 80
Garbo, Greta, 78, 79
Garland, Judy, 82
George V, 26-7, 76, 77, 94-7, 102
George VI, 103, 105, 107
George, Prince, Duke of Kent, 76-7
Gloucester, Duke of, 103
Geobbels, Dr, 99, 113
Goering, Hermann, 99, 108
Gold Standard, 13, 16-17
Golf, 88
Gollancz, Victor, 42, 44
Grandi, Count, 117
Graves, Robert, 8, 93
Greene, Graham, 89
Guernica, bombing of, 44, 113

Hagen, Walter, 88
Haile Selassie, Emperor, 99-100, 121
Halifax, Lord, 108, 117
Hall, Henry, 56, 79
Hardie, Keir, 59
Harrisson, Tom, 74
Henderson, Sir Neville, 119
Henry, John, 78
Hepworth, Barbara, 49
Hibberd, Stuart, 102
Hiking, 74-5
Hiller, Wendy, 80
Hindenburg, President, 65
Hitler, Adolf, 62-5, 85, 86, 87, 99, 100-101, 108, 113, 117-21, 122, 123-7
Hoare, Sir Samuel, 98-9, 100, 117, 123
Hobbs, Jack, 85
Hollywood, *see also* Cinema, 21, 78-83
Hore-Belisha, Leslie, 114, 122
Housing, 13-14, 21, 29, 33, 54-7
Howard, Leslie, 80
Huxley, Aldous, 89, 90

Independent Labour Party, 62
Inskip, Sir Thomas, 117
Intelligentsia, the, 40-50, 74
Interior decoration, 51-8
International Brigade, 110-13
Invergordon, Mutiny of, 14-17
Isherwood, Christopher, 41

Jardine, D. R., 86
Jarrow March, 66-9
John, Augustus, 48
Johnson, Amy, 83-5
Johnson, Dean Hewlett, 42
Jones, Bobby, 88
Joyce, James, 90
Jubilee, Silver, 94-7
Jung, Carl, 46

Kauffer, McKnight, 45, 48, 55
Keitel, General, 119
Keynes, Maynard, 61
Kredit Anstalt Bank, 12

Labour Party, 10, 12, 14, 17, 62, 112
Lansbury, George, 62, 63
Larwood, H., 86

Laughton, Charles, 80
Laurel and Hardy, 80, 82
Laval, Pierre, 98
Law, A. Bonar, 61
Lawrence, D. H., 46, 47, 89
League of Nations, 99-100, 112
Left Book Club, 44, 93
Lewis, Wyndham, 48
Libraries, Circulating, 88-9
Liddell Hart, Basil, 61-2
Light industries, 21-2
Lindberg, Charles, 83
Lloyd George, David, 61
Louis, Joe, 86
Low, David, 99
Ludendorff, General, 63
Luxembourg, Radio, 78

MacDonald, Jeanette, 80
MacDonald, Ramsay, 12, 13, 15, 17, 23 26, 59, 66, 68, 95
Macmillan, Harold, 117
MacNeice, Louis, 40, 49-50, 112
MacPherson, Sandy, 78
Madge, Charles, 74
Maginot line, 114, 120
Magritte, René, 109
Manders, John, 65
Marble, Alice, 88
Marches (hunger and protest), 66-72
Margaret, Princess, 105, 107
Marina, Princess, 76-7
Marshall, Herbert, 79-80
Marshall, Howard, 76
Marx Brothers, 82
Marx, Groucho, 11
Marxism, *see also* Communism, 42-6, 48, 49, 112
Mary, Queen, 94, 102
Maschwitz, Eric, 76-7
Mass Observation, 74
Matthews, Stanley, 85
Maugham, W. Somerset, 92
Maxton, James, 59, 62
Means Test, 17-20
Middleton, Mr, 78
Mollison, Jim, 84-5
Moore, Henry, 49
Mosley, Oswald, 62, 69-72, 75, 107
Mowrer, Edgar, 93
Munich Agreement, 121, 122, 123-7
Murdoch, Richard, 78
Mussolini, Benito, 72, 95, 99, 108, 112-13, 117
Mussolini, Bruno, 95

Nash, Paul, 48
National Government, 14, 15, 23, 59
Neagle, Anna, 77
Nicholson, Ben, 48
Nuthall, Betty, 85

Oldfield, W. A., 86
Olympic Games, 86-7
Orwell, George, 20, 43, 104
Owens, Jesse, 86-7
Oxford Group, 74

Papen, von, 65
Payne, Jack, 56
Perry, Fred, 88
Picasso, Pablo, 44, 48, 49, 113
Porter, Cole, 79
Powell, William, 80
Priestley, J. B., 92, 93
Public Assistance, 20

Quennell, Peter, 44

Read, Herbert, 48
Reading, Lord, 15
Refugees, 114-15, 116
Reith, Sir John, 76, 78
Remarque, Erich, 9
Rhineland, Occupation of, 101
Ribbentrop, J. von, 54, 119
Robeson, Paul, 42
Rogers, Ginger, 79, 80, 81
Roosevelt, Franklin D., 62
Rotha, Paul, 74
Rothermere, Lord, 107
Rothschild, Baron Eugene de, 107
Runciman, Walter, 67-9, 118
Russell, Bertrand, 92

Sarazen, Gene, 88

Sayers, Dorothy, 89
Schmelling, Max, 86
Segrave, Sir Henry, 87
Shaw, Bernard, 92
Sherriff, R. C., 9
Shirach, Baldur von, 72
Simon, Sir John, 117
Simpson, Ernest, 105, 106
Simpson, Mrs Wallis, 104-7
Snagge, John, 76, 78
Snowden, Philip, 14, 15
Spades, Ace of, 28
Spanish Civil War, 109-13, 114, 117
Spencer, Stanley, 48
Spender, Stephen, 40, 112
Stack, Prunella, 73-4
Stone, Christopher, 78
Strachey, John, 62
Strachey, Lytton, 93
Strike, the General, 10
Sudetenland Crisis, 118-21
Surrealism, 48, 108-9
Sutherland, Graham, 48-9

Tauber, Richard, 28, 39, 78
Taylor, Robert, 80
Temple, Shirley, 80, 82
Tennis, 85, 87-8
Thomas, J. H., 12, 15, 62
Twenties, the, 7-11, 37, 47, 58, 92

Unemployment, 6, 10, 12, 13, 14, 15, 17-21, 24, 33, 108

Versailles, Treaty of, 63, 101, 117
Voce, W., 86

Wales, Prince of, *see also* Edward VIII and Duke of Windsor, 28, 37, 102
Wall Street Crash, 7, 11, 12
Wandervogel, 72
Waugh, Evelyn, 90-2
Webb, Mary, 39
Weimar Republic, 64
Wells, H. G., 10, 92
West, Mae, 80
Western Brothers, the, 78
Wilkinson, Ellen, 68-9
Wills, Helen, 88
Windsor, Duke of, *see also* Prince of Wales and Edward VIII, 107
Wodehouse, P. G., 92
Women's League of Health and Beauty, 73-4
Woodfull, W. M., 86

Yeats, W. B., 92

Zog, King of Albania, 123